The GAME COOK

The GAME COOK

Inspired Recipes for
Pheasant, Partridge,
Duck, Deer, Rabbit,
and More

NORMAN TEBBIT

LYONS PRESS
Guilford, Connecticut
An imprint of Globe Pequot Press

To my wife, Margaret, who has guided and sustained my efforts in the kitchen for more than half a century.

Lyons Press is an imprint of Globe Pequot Press.

Illustrations © Debby Mason www.debbymason.com

Text design: Nancy Freeborn

Library of Congress Cataloging-in-Publication Data is available on file.

ISBN 978-0-7627-7048-9

Printed in the United States of America

10 9 8 7 6 5 4 3 2 1

CONTENTS

Acknowledgments

To Beryl Goldsmith, who typed every page of the manuscript, mostly several times over; the Aylings, father and son, of the New Street Butchers, Horsham; Michel George, whose Belgian connections imported the recipe for rabbit with prunes; Jeremy Ashpool of Jeremy's Restaurant, Borde Hill, who contributed one of his favorite venison recipes; Debby Mason, my illustrator, who also contributed some of her recipes; and all my shooting friends who have helped me provide the birds and beasts for these recipes.

INSPIRATION

Game in the Kitchen

THIS BOOK WAS INSPIRED BY A CONVERSATION IN MY FAVORITE butcher's shop. I commented that I noticed that many people bought rubber-boned, tasteless chicken in supermarkets rather than good-quality pheasants for less. "Why do they do it?" I asked. "They even pay twice the price if the label for the poor creature says 'organic' or 'free range.' And surely the life of a game bird is better than that of such chickens."

"Mostly," said the butcher, "because they have never cooked game. They think it is difficult, tastes strange, and they wouldn't like it." The more I thought about it and the more people I asked, the more I believed he was right. We tried putting photocopies of my favorite ways of cooking pheasants on his counter and found they helped to sell pheasants.

I decided to write about game. Not only about cooking it, but also about game itself and why it is good food. As for the cooking, well cooking is not a science. I enjoy cooking, and it should not be a chore. I am a great admirer of Delia Smith's cookbooks. If you have never even boiled an egg, stand to attention, open her book, and briskly (without hesitation or deviation) do exactly as she orders, and even complicated recipes turn out well. I admire Jane Grigson, too. As for her daughter, Sophie, I am also a fervent admirer.

I have tried to steer a middle course between these titans of the kitchen. These recipes will work if you follow them, but they are not sacred texts. I hope you will try them—then vary them and make them your own, and there is room at the end of the book for your own notes. My own cookbooks are covered in notes—"needs more cream" or "double the amount of chutney."

I should make it clear that I learned only basic cooking at my mother's knee. Then in my airplane flying days I was often away for two or three weeks at a time, then at home for a week or more. When I was at home I shared domestic duties with my wife, who taught me to be a more adventurous cook. For the past twenty-five years, since Sinn Fein/IRA terrorists almost murdered us both and left her crippled, I have been the family cook—assisted by advice from the wheelchair.

My gurus of the kitchen had been the Grigsons, Carrier, and, of course, Delia Smith. No kitchen should be without Smith's *Complete Illustrated Cookery Course* or Sophie Grigson's *Meat Course, Fish Course,* and *Eat Your Greens.* Jane Grigson's *English Food,* Elizabeth David's *French Provincial Cooking,* and Joyce Molyneux's *Carved Angel Cookery Book* should also be on the shelf, and for fun, the *Two Fat Ladies: Gastronomic Adventures* (whose fish pie is the greatest).

With a few exceptions (mayonnaise and soufflés, for example), you should not have to stick precisely to quantities. My recipe for pheasants and cream is just one of hundreds of variations on that classic dish. Make it the way that pleases you. Try it with Cointreau rather than Calvados, green or red apples, peeled or not, and have a glass of Sancerre for the cook along the way.

Enjoy cooking as well as eating. Enjoy this book as much as I have enjoyed experimenting in the kitchen and writing it. The illustrations are by Debby Mason, who created the mezzotint plates from which they were printed. Sometimes called "half tone," mezzotints were invented by Ludwig von Siegen in the seventeenth century. Mezzotints are produced on copper plates. The entire surface of the plate is roughed with a tool—the mezzotint rocker—shaped like a wide chisel with a curved and serrated edge. By rocking the toothed edge backward and forward over the plate, a rough burr is cast up that holds the ink. Once completed, a drawing can be transferred onto the plate with carbon paper. When printed, this textured ground reads as a uniform dark; the areas to be lightened are scraped and burnished—therefore working from dark to light.

The preparation of the plate can take fifteen hours or more before the artist can start work on the design, but the beautiful, soft velvety finish is so unique to the mezzotint process that it more than justifies the skill and patience involved. In the eighteenth century small boys were employed to "rock" the plates up, and the extreme tediousness of the work, combined with the poor pay and working conditions, sent many of the poor things into mental decline, hence the term "off one's rocker."

SO WHAT IS GAME?

STRICTLY SPEAKING, GAME IS ANY ANIMAL OR BIRD LIVING wild that is hunted for food. By convention, game is divided into three categories: small birds, such as quail; then birds such as grouse, partridge, pheasant, and duck, as well as rabbit and hare; and finally larger game, which includes deer, wild boar, and in some parts of the world, bear.

Of course most of us would not share the Mediterranean passion for killing and eating songbirds, and if you want to roast a bear, you are on your own as far as I am concerned. What's more, although most partridges and pheasants are not fully wild, in that they are protected by gamekeepers and may be hatched in pens before released into the wild, they are neither kept captive in sheds nor slaughtered like Bernard Matthews's turkeys at the end of their brief lives.

The secret of the superior texture and flavor of game is that the creatures have lived as fully functional wild animals. They are not dosed with food and confined to a pen or shed. Although pheasant in particular often have the benefit of food being supplied by their keepers, that is as much to keep them from wandering off on to someone else's land as to feed them. They are free of (and need to) forage for their own food. If you can distinguish between the rubber debeaked chicken that has never seen sunshine, been showered by rain, or felt grass under its feet before its life ended at six weeks or less, and a "free-range" bird confined to a yard outside its barn, then you will certainly appreciate the meat of a bird that has flown and run free through woods and fields. And what a difference there is between those pallid, long, frozen Chinese rabbits and the real thing that has lived, loved, and feasted on my roses or my farming friends' carrots.

I am not too sure that I would be able to tell the difference between top-quality farmed venison and the truly wild meat, so do not lightly refuse to use the farmed variety if the wild is not on your butcher's slab.

Traditionally, game excludes fish—despite the expression "game fish." This book does not take quite such a narrow view. Anyway, almost all the fish we eat is wild and has been hunted and caught—and very good it is too—but I have confined my recipes to those for that fish of fish, the salmon—and I have also included scallops, because my illustrator, Debby Mason, goes scuba diving for them. In short, for me, to be game it must have lived free and been hunted, trapped, hooked, or shot, whether it be feathered, furred or scaly, or in a shell.

These days you may well find game on the shelves of your supermarket, and it may well be of decent quality and reasonable price. My advice, however, is to find a good butcher, get to know him, tell him what you want, trust his judgment—and never forget to tell him if what you bought was good or bad.

USEFUL TIPS

Kit For The Kitchen

I am sure you have your own favorite pieces of kitchen equipment, and I would not want to tell you how to equip your kitchen—but there are some things that you really need in order to make game cooking easy. These are my favorite and much-used items:

- A really good-quality 10- to 11-inch double-handled, stainless-steel pan about 4 inches deep with a well-fitting lid.

- Two large (10- to 11-inch) frying pans, one stainless steel and one non-stick. I do not use nonstick pans a lot (for one thing you cannot scrape at them with a stainless-steel spatula) but now and again they are really useful.

- At least one smaller stainless-steel frying pan.

- It always pays to buy the best-quality casserole pans, and I do not think there are any better than Le Creuset. I have a couple of round ones—8 inches—and a couple of oval ones—11 x 9 inches. The lids fit so well and they hold heat very well, and like stainless-steel pans they are easy to clean. (If for any reason your pans have lids that do not fit tightly, use a piece of kitchen foil under the lid to seal in all the moisture so that it doesn't evaporate.) Nor would I like to be without my Le Creuset griddle.

- A roasting pan, a good rack for it, and several lightweight coated baking sheets or very shallow baking trays (about ¼ inch deep).

- I also have a large and small brown earthenware casserole.

- Among the odds and ends, I value my poultry scissors, three or four wooden spoons, a good stainless-steel fish slice, and a couple of plastic fish slices to use on coated surfaces.

- I also have a good selection of knives.

I realize that our kitchen is very well equipped, but it has taken my wife and I over fifty years and goodness knows how much money to build it up. Our advice to anyone starting from scratch is to buy the best—and if you cannot afford that, buy something cheap (then, when you can afford quality, you will not feel bad about throwing the old one out or using it in the garden). The mistake is to spend almost as much as the best would cost and feel it is not good enough—but also feel that it cost too much to throw out.

Planning Ahead

Many of the recipes here are roasts, and one of the perennial problems with a roast, apart from making sure that the joint and any trimmings plus all the vegetables are ready at the same time, is making sure that you have hot serving dishes and plates ready when you need them. As soon as the meat is carved, it will start to cool, and if it is then put onto cold plates, even hot gravy will not be enough to remedy the sorry situation. To avoid this, plan ahead. If you have a range, then the warming oven will be perfect. If you have a double oven, the main oven can be set on high for the roast and the second oven on a lower heat for the plates and dishes. Things get more complicated when you have just one oven. If you take the joint out of the oven to rest before carving, leave the oven door slightly ajar to reduce the heat and put plates and dishes inside to warm. If all the food is coming out of the oven at the same time, then be resourceful: Fill a clean sink with boiling water and immerse the plates in that; put them in the microwave (if they are microwave proof); use a microwave-heated plate warmer; stand them on a heat tray . . . you get the idea.

Jointing a Pheasant or Partridge

The structure of most game birds is about the same as that of chickens. However, I still find ducks and geese a bit puzzling when I am carving them, as the legs are designed as much for swimming as for walking. But with only a little swearing, I usually get it about right. The main thing is not to be intimidated by either the bird itself or the kitchen bystanders, who should be told to go and do the washing up—or pour the cook a glass of wine.

You do need a sharp knife—not too long; I would suggest about 4 to 6 inches—and a pair of poultry scissors or shears. My mother's father, who was a butcher, maintained that you are far more likely to cut yourself using a blunt knife than a sharp one, and I think he was right.

Always start with the bird on its back on a good wooden board. The first thing to do is to remove the legs. If you simply hold the bird firmly down onto the board with one hand and pull a leg out and down away from the body with the other, you will feel where the top joint (the hip) joins the main skeleton. If it is a young and tender one, you may feel the hip joint dislocate. Cut down through the stretched skin and the knife will more or less find its own way down to the joint. A little pressure and you will find yourself through the meat and looking at the joint. Press the leg out again, and the joint will fully dislocate. Flushed with success, cut down through the rest of the skin and meat and put the first leg to one side. Now turn the bird around and do the same again.

Next, slide your knife down along the breastbone to separate it from the meat on one side of the bone. With a bit of practice you will find this quite easy (and you will leave less and less meat on the breastbone). Continue separating the breast meat right down from the ribs and backbone. Turn the bird around and separate the other breast. You now have four pieces: two legs and two breasts with the wings attached.

On a chicken your next move is to remove the bony little outer winglets with the scissors or shears. Very often you will find that they were removed when the bird was plucked. Indeed, there is not a lot of meat on a partridge or small pheasant wing, and the plucker may have already removed them. Sometimes most of one wing may have gone if it took a heavy load of shot, came down heavily, or was retrieved by an over-enthusiastic Labrador.

Trim the parson's nose off the carcass. Now, to make six pieces you will need to divide each breast. This is a matter of judgment to get a fair division between a smaller piece of breast with the leg (which does not have much meat on it) and a larger piece of just breast.

Stock

There are quite a few myths about making stock. However, stock as used in the recipes in *The Game Cook* are really quite simple and straightforward. The ingredients are quite variable according to whether you are making stock from the carcasses of game birds or from those of rabbits, hares, or deer.

The basic method is to bring the carcass and any giblets (kidneys, liver, and so on) and some vegetable pieces (onion, carrot, celery, and so on), some herbs (parsley, thyme, basil, tarragon), and seasoning (salt, black pepper, and peppercorns) together in a saucepan with about 1.5 cups of cold water per bird and more according to size. Bring it all to a boil briefly with the lid on the pan, then turn it down to simmer for 30 minutes.

Any spare stock can be frozen for later use. I find that ice-cube containers are useful; I turn the cubes out and keep them in a freezer bag.

Pheasant, Partridge, Pigeon Stock

The carcass and any bits of 1 bird

2 pints water

6 black peppercorns

3 twigs fresh thyme or 1 teaspoon dried thyme

3 sprigs parsley

Other herbs, such as basil, tarragon, etc., to taste

Salt, to taste

Break the carcass into 2 or 3 pieces and put them in a saucepan with the water, peppercorns, thyme, parsley, other herbs, and salt. Bring to a boil, turn heat down to simmer, and simmer with the lid on for 30 minutes. Strain the stock into a suitable container and discard the remainder.

Rabbit, Hare, or Venison Stock

1 carcass, with heart, liver, and/or kidneys if not used elsewhere

6–12 black peppercorns according to the size of the carcass

6 twigs fresh thyme

6 sprigs parsley

Other herbs, such as basil and especially tarragon, to taste

3 cups cold water

Place all the ingredients in a saucepan and cover. Bring the mixture to a brief boil, turn the heat down to simmer, and then simmer for 45 minutes to 1 hour according to the size of the carcass. Strain the stock into a suitable container and discard the remainder.

Beurre Manié

A beurre manié is simply a paste of equal amounts of butter and flour. All you do is soften the butter over low heat in a saucepan, add the flour a little at a time, and mix with a wooden spoon to a really stiff paste. It needs to be a bit softer than Blu-Tack (which is a putty-like adhesive).

You will not often need very much, and I suggest that unless a recipe calls specifically for more, you should use no more than 2 ounces each of flour and butter. Usually you will be adding this to stock, sauce, or gravy to thicken it, so I would add it in lumps about the size of a thumbnail.

Some recipes will suggest you use onion as well as the butter and flour. In this case cut about ¼ cup of onion into very thin slices. Fry gently until soft in 4 tablespoons of butter and then add the flour as above.

Bouquet Garni

This is just a handy way to use herbs to add flavor without leaving stalks of thyme and bedraggled-looking parsley or bay leaves in the dish. You could also cheat and buy a packet of bouquet garni of mixed dried crushed herbs in bags like tea bags.

The other way to go is to decide which fresh herbs would go best in the dish you are preparing—very often this is thyme, coriander, parsley, basil, and oregano. Cut fairly long stalks of each herb (2 inches or so), wrap them around a bay leaf, and then tie everything firmly together with string.

Mashed Potatoes & Celeriac

Don't use anything but good potatoes and choose your celeriac carefully. There can be a lot of waste when you peel it, and if you get an old or not very fresh one, you may find the center a bit fluffy. If so, discard those bits. However, it is best if you keep reasonably close to a ratio of 2 to 1 celeriac to potato.

> 1 pound potatoes
>
> 2 pounds celeriac
>
> 2–3 garlic cloves, to taste
>
> 4 tablespoons butter
>
> ⅓ cup thick cream
>
> Salt and pepper to taste

1. Peel the potatoes, dice them into 1-inch cubes, and then place them in a saucepan of cold water. Peel the celeriac, discarding the root pieces and any "fluffy" bits in the center. Dice it into 1-inch cubes and put in a saucepan of cold water.

2. Drain off both the potatoes and celeriac, give them fresh water, and cook in separate saucepans, bringing them to a boil, then turning them down to a fast simmer (adding the garlic to the potatoes). This should take about 10 minutes. You want them soft but not mushy.

3. When cooked, put the potatoes and celeriac together in a bowl big enough to use a handheld electric mixer in. Start to mix them and, as the lumps break up, chop the butter into bits and add it and the cream to the potatoes and celeriac. Continue to mix until you get a nice smooth paste. Season with salt and pepper.

PHEASANT

[Phasianus colchicus]

*Like all game, you will not find much fat
on a pheasant—certainly not until around
Christmas after they have been stuffing
themselves with acorns.*

A GOOD WELL-GROWN COCK BIRD may have a wingspan of three feet and weigh five pounds or more. Although pheasants are well able to survive anywhere they can find seeds, grain shoots, and acorns for food; cover for their ground nests; and good roosting spots on the edges of woods, their natural population is hugely increased by the release in the spring of young birds that have been raised and protected by gamekeepers.

Once you have your bird in the kitchen, note that anything you can do with a chicken you can do with a pheasant—and then some. Unlike a chicken, a pheasant (and almost all game) does need to be hung for its flesh to tenderize and the full flavor to develop. That presents some problems these days, as there are those who decree that once shot, your game birds must be kept in a cooler at a temperature no higher than 40°F. At that temperature it needs at least ten days before the bird is cleaned. Oh—and do not worry about lead shot: It rarely stops in the flesh of the bird, and if it does, it will not poison you. Bottom-feeding waterfowl are at risk because lead pellets accumulate in their crops—but humans do not have crops, so the lead does not hang around in our digestive system.

As with all game, you will not find much fat on a pheasant so I generally casserole rather than roast them. As ever, cooking a bird in a casserole could not be more straightforward, but it is the quality of fruit, vegetables, other meats, wine, cider, and spirits that turn a decent bird into a magnificent meal.

Pheasant with Apples & Cream

[Faisan à la Normande]

This is my favorite way to cook pheasant. It is a classic casseroled dish that depends not just on the quality of the bird but also on the fruit, vegetables, and other ingredients you use. A good fat pheasant (cock or hen) will feed just four adults. Use a brace if you have hungry teenagers, but then double all the quantities below.

I like to prepare this dish early in the day and cook it until it is all but done, then take it out of the oven and return it again to a hot oven for the last thirty to forty minutes.

It is hard to select vegetables to serve with this dish. Baked potatoes are great, but you will need two ovens, as they need to cook at about 400°F (don't be tempted to compromise by cooking the bird and potatoes at the midway point of 350°F—it spoils both), and I do not like potatoes cooked in the microwave. Mashed potatoes are good, perhaps cooked with celeriac, as are roasted or mashed parsnips, or broccoli.

> 2 tablespoons butter
>
> 1–2 tablespoons olive oil
>
> 1 good, fat, well-hung pheasant
>
> 1 onion, chopped
>
> 1 4-ounce piece fat belly of pork, cut into 4 pieces, or unsmoked bacon slices, cut into ¼-inch pieces
>
> 6 tart apples, peeled if the skins are tough, cored, and fairly thickly sliced
>
> ⅝ cup heavy cream
>
> 1–2 tablespoons Calvados or Cointreau
>
> 1–2 tablespoons dry white wine or water
>
> A little ground cinnamon (optional)
>
> Salt and freshly ground black pepper

1. Preheat the oven to 325°F.

2. Heat the butter and oil in a large stainless steel pan and brown the pheasant all over. Once the bird is browned, put it in a lidded casserole, put on the lid, and keep warm in the oven.

3. Fry the onion and pork belly lightly in the fat remaining in the pan. If need be, add a touch more oil, but do not overdo it. Remove the onion and pork and keep warm with the pheasant. Add the apples to the pan and fry lightly until they just begin to soften, then remove and keep separate from the bird, pork, and onions.

4. Return the bird, pork, and onions to the pan and fry briefly again and then return them to the casserole dish. Add the apples and cream to the casserole, the Calvados (or, if you have a sweet tooth, you can use Cointreau, although I prefer the apple dryness of Calvados).

5. I like to take up all the brown bits sticking to the bottom of the pan with 1 tablespoon or so of dry white wine or water, scraping it out with a stainless steel spatula as it comes to a boil, then adding them to the casserole. If you like cinnamon, you may want to sprinkle a very little on the apples. Add some pepper and, if you wish, a little salt. Make sure the casserole lid fits tightly (if need be, put a piece of aluminum foil under it) and return it to the oven for about 2 hours, though the timing will vary with the age, size, and quality of the bird. You will find that when it is almost done, the legs will have begun to fall away from the body. Toward the end of the cooking time, put a serving dish in the oven to warm.

6. When all is done and everyone is seated at the table, put the bird on the serving dish. If you prefer a smooth sauce, then blend the remaining ingredients in the casserole with a handheld blender (personally I like it with a slightly lumpy texture). Either way, pour some over the bird and put the rest in a jug to pass around.

Pheasant with Red Cabbage

This is a classic recipe and a good way to stretch a pheasant to provide a meal for four people, or even six with the addition of sausages to the red cabbage. Cooking pheasant is absolutely straightforward, apart, that is, from jointing the bird, which takes a bit of practice, but your butcher should do it for you—or show you how to do it. Failing that, see page xiv for DIY instructions.

It is really a complete dish served straight from the casserole. The most important thing is to get the red cabbage right. After that everything else falls into place. Of course, if you are feeding teenagers, then baked potatoes would not go amiss. But if you want to impress dinner guests, Sophie Grigson, in her version of this classic recipe, suggests that you lay it all out smartly on a big oval serving dish.

1 large red cabbage, cored and shredded

Tart apples (use half the weight of the cabbage), cored and sliced

Onions (use the same weight as the apples), sliced

¼ cup raisins

3 tablespoons brown sugar

1 garlic clove, finely chopped or crushed

¼–½ teaspoon ground cinnamon

¼–½ teaspoon freshly grated nutmeg

Salt and freshly ground black pepper

2–3 tablespoons red wine vinegar

Juice of 1 orange

1¼ cups red wine

1 tablespoon olive or sunflower oil

1 pound pork chipolata sausages (optional)

2 good, fat, well-hung pheasants, each jointed into 4 pieces

1. Preheat the oven to 300°F.

2. Put the shredded cabbage, apples, onions, raisins, sugar, garlic, spices and some salt and pepper in layers in a large lidded casserole dish (preferably Le Creuset). Pour the wine vinegar, orange juice, and red wine into a measuring cup and add water to make 2 cups. Pour liquid over the cabbage. Put on the casserole lid and cook in the preheated oven for about 2 hours. Take a look after 1 hour to make sure it is not getting dry. If it is, add some more water or wine.

3. Once you have checked the cabbage, heat the oil in a frying pan. If you are using sausages, prick them thoroughly and then fry until they are half cooked. Remove from the pan with a slotted spoon and reserve, then brown the pheasant pieces in the fat and oil. Push the pheasant pieces and sausages well down into the cabbage. You can, if you think the juices from cooking them are not too greasy, pour them on top of the cabbage—that is just a matter of taste. Return the casserole to the oven for another 2 hours, by which time the pheasant will be thoroughly cooked.

Easiest-Ever Curried Pheasant with Dhal

Curries are often used as a way to use up leftover roast meat. Personally, I do not think that is the best way to make a curry, or perhaps to use leftovers, and on page 23 you will find a recipe for deviled pheasant (adapted from the usual post-Christmas deviled turkey).

If, however, you are looking at leftover pheasant, then hopefully you have a jar of Patak's excellent korma sauce in the cupboard. There is nothing wrong with simply following the instructions on the jar, but I would lightly fry an onion and a chopped garlic clove; add the meat, chopped into bite-size pieces; fry it all up together; keep it hot; and then simply add the sauce as instructed on the label. Then heat it all through, put it into a casserole, and cook it in the oven for 30–40 minutes at about 325°F.

Alternatively, if you are going to curry an uncooked bird, you should follow the recipe below. If you want to keep the pheasant in large pieces, it is best to almost cook it one day, leave the meat to absorb the spices overnight, and then finish cooking it the next day. In my opinion, any curry is best if it has been left to absorb all the flavors into the meat (or fish) and then reheated, otherwise it can sometimes taste like curry sauce with bits of meat (or fish) in it. If you want to eat right away, however, you need to cut the meat into smaller pieces.

Serve the curry with plain rice. There are so many "proper" ways to cook rice that I think it is easiest to follow the instructions on the package—but do buy good-quality Indian Patna rice. Make sure you warm a dish in the oven shortly before you need it. Put just a little butter or oil in the bottom, and, if you let the rice drain well before putting it in the dish, and then turn it just once to coat it with the butter, it should turn out well.

I also like to have dhal with curry, which is why I've provided a recipe for it. It is ideal if you have a hungry family. It also freezes well, so you may wish to make some extra to freeze, ready for the next curry. Add some good mango chutney and some poppadoms, naan bread, or chapatis to make an excellent meal.

Pheasant

1 tablespoon olive oil or 4 tablespoons butter

1 medium onion, finely chopped

2 garlic cloves, finely chopped

1 good, fat, well-hung pheasant, jointed into 4 pieces (see page xiv)

1 jar (at least) Patak's curry sauce, or similar

Dhal

8 ounces lentils (the large green ones are best), soaked in water for 1–2 hours, or overnight if more convenient

½ teaspoon ground turmeric

½ teaspoon chili powder (or to taste)

Salt (optional)

1–2 tablespoons olive oil or 2 tablespoons butter

1 8-ounce can chopped tomatoes, or 3 or 4 fresh tomatoes, skinned

2 medium onions, finely chopped

1. Heat the oil or melt the butter in a frying pan and fry the onions and garlic gently until golden. Add the pheasant pieces. Stir in the curry sauce with a wooden spoon and continue frying for another 3–4 minutes or until they are browned. Put the pieces into a casserole dish and cook in the oven at 325°F until done (1½–2 hours).

2. About 45 minutes before the pheasant will be ready, prepare the dhal. Put the soaked lentils into about 2½ cups boiling water with the turmeric and chili (and a little salt if you wish), bring to a boil, and then simmer for around 30 minutes, until tender.

3. In the meantime, heat the oil until golden, then add the tomatoes and onions and cook for a little longer. Add these to the cooked lentils and cook for another 5–10 minutes, until the dhal is about the consistency of porridge. Serve with the pheasant.

Roast Pheasant

The pheasant is a wild bird, so it carries less fat than a chicken, particularly early in the season, and it needs roasting with care. Generally speaking the hen bird, though smaller, will roast better than the cock, but in any case I would rather roast pheasant in December or January than in October. It is also important to be sure that your butcher hangs the bird for at least six to seven days (and not in a freezing-cold room!) before it is cleaned.

As always, whether roasting a chicken or game bird, the stuffing is important. Game birds need stuffings that contain fat (none of your bread crumbs; something more like blood sausage—even haggis—or a steak fillet), and you will need good, fat, unsmoked bacon or sheets of pork fat to keep the bird well basted. As an alternative to using just strips of steak as a stuffing, you could try either the blood sausage and oatmeal stuffing or the fruit-based stuffing below. (The former is a recent invention, and I am still adjusting the amount of herbs to get it just right for my taste, but I include the basic recipe from which you can work.)

As far as vegetables are concerned, I like this with traditional winter fare: mashed rutabaga, shredded buttered cabbage, or perhaps roast parsnips or mashed potatoes with celeriac. I often serve potatoes cooked as my wife used to do, in the recipe below.

> 1 good, fat, well-hung pheasant
>
> ½ tablespoon butter
>
> 1 2-ounce piece fillet steak (or stuffing—see below)
>
> Fat, unsmoked bacon or sheets of pork fat—enough to cover the pheasant

For the Blood Sausage Stuffing

4 ounces blood sausage or haggis

3 ounces oatmeal or fresh white bread crumbs

1 small apple, chopped

1 heaping teaspoon chopped thyme

½ teaspoon chopped parsley

1 egg, beaten

1 teaspoon brandy

Salt and freshly ground black pepper

For the Fruit Stuffing

1 apple, quartered

Chopped plums or ready-to-eat dried apricots or prunes or dates—
  enough to stuff the bird

4 ounces fresh white bread crumbs

About ½ tablespoon butter

For the Gravy

1 small carrot, sliced

1 stalk celery, sliced

1 small onion or 2 shallots, halved

1 bouquet garni (see page xvii)

½ cup game bird stock (see page xvi) or chicken stock

A little white flour, for thickening

1 glass red wine

For the Sliced Roasted Potatoes

Enough potatoes for 4 people

A little oil

1. Preheat the oven to 400°F.

2. Thoroughly butter the cavity of the bird and put the steak inside, cut into strips, or use one of the stuffings.

3. For the blood sausage stuffing, mix the chopped up blood sausage or haggis, oatmeal or bread crumbs, chopped apples, and herbs together in a bowl. Then add the beaten egg, brandy, and plenty of salt and pepper. Transfer to a saucepan and gently warm it all until it is hot before using it to stuff the bird. (My illustrator, Debby Mason, favors a good slug of whiskey to go with the haggis to make this a "Flying Scotsman Pheasant.")

4. If you prefer the fruit stuffing, chop and thoroughly mix all the ingredients in a bowl, transfer to a saucepan, warm thoroughly until hot, and then use to stuff the bird. Remember that tightly stuffing a bird with a big blob of cold stuffing will extend the cooking time by 20 minutes or even more, so it is well worth getting it hot first.

5. Cover the pheasant well with the bacon, using cocktail sticks to keep it in position.

6. For the gravy, put the carrots, celery, onions, and bouquet garni in a roasting pan and place a roasting rack on top. Add a little hot water, just ¼ inch or so, which, together with some bird or chicken stock, will be the base of the gravy.

7. Place the pheasant on the rack and place it in the oven. The pheasant will take 45–60 minutes (according to age and size), although a 2-year-old bird might take longer. Check to see if it is done from time to time (the juices will run clear and the legs will be falling away) and add a little more hot water if need be to keep the vegetables from drying out.

8. For the sliced roasted potatoes, put the potatoes in a saucepan and cover with cold water. Bring to a boil to scald the potatoes and then drain and slice thinly. Place the potatoes in two layers in a lightly oiled ovenproof dish, drizzling a little oil over each layer, and put in the oven with the pheasant for the remaining half an hour of the cooking time, until nicely brown, turning over if need be to make sure they are all a bit crisp.

9. About 15 minutes before the pheasant will be ready, remove the bacon from the skin to crispen it. Leave the bacon in the oven so it keeps warm for serving with the bird—or if the children (or even guests) are beginning to turn nasty while waiting for food, buy them off with the crispy bacon bits.

10. When the pheasant is done, remove it to a dish in a warming or second oven, if you have one. If not, turn the oven off and put the pheasant on a warm serving dish wrapped in aluminum foil and leave it to rest.

11. Lift out the vegetable bits from the roasting pan with a slotted spoon (I think they are too good to waste, and I serve them with the bird). Put the roasting pan on the stove and add some of the bird or chicken stock. Turn up the heat to bring to a boil and scrape all the bits from the bottom of the pan with a wooden spoon. Sprinkle in a bit of flour a little at a time, and keep stirring to work out any lumps. Add the red wine and use as much stock as you need to make as much gravy as you like, stirring all the while with a wooden spoon until the gravy has thickened. Add the salt and pepper and all is ready.

Simple Casseroled Pheasant

The basic casseroled pheasant (or most other meats) is a simple enough affair. You fry some onions or shallots and pork or bacon, put them on one side, brown the bird in the oil and juices, put it all in a casserole dish, add stock and wine, then cook it all at 325°F until done (1–1½ hours). That is pretty straightforward, and the art of making it into a really fine meal lies in the extras: mushrooms, apples, cabbage, cream, and so on (but not all together, needless to say). A good fat pheasant will be enough for four people, unless they are teenagers.

If you are going overboard when serving this dish, you could have croutons around it to decorate the dish. As for vegetables, I like baked potatoes, but if you have only one oven, then this is a problem, as I think the potatoes need to be cooked at 400°F (and the microwave just makes them soggy). Mashed potatoes or mashed potatoes and celeriac is good, mashed rutabaga gives extra color, and I would never turn my nose up at broccoli, provided it is steaming hot and not overcooked.

1–2 tablespoons olive oil or 1 tablespoon butter

1 good, fat, well-hung pheasant

1 4-ounce piece fat belly of pork or unsmoked bacon, cut into 4 pieces

1 cup small onions or shallots

Glass of red or white wine

1¼ cup pheasant stock (see page xvi) or chicken stock

1 bouquet garni (see page xvii)

Salt and freshly ground black pepper

8 ounces portabellini or field mushrooms

A little plain flour, for thickening (optional)

1 tablespoon redcurrant jelly (optional)

1. Preheat the oven to 325°F. Heat half the oil or melt half the butter in a frying pan and brown the pheasant on all sides. Transfer it into a lidded casserole dish (preferably Le Creuset) using a slotted spoon and keep warm in the oven.

2. Sauté the pork belly or bacon in the fat remaining in the pan and, as the fat begins to flow, add the onions or shallots and fry until golden. Use the other half of the oil or butter if needed.

3. Return the bird to the pan, let it all warm up, then pour in the wine and let it sizzle and bubble for a moment or 2 before adding the stock and bouquet garni and seasoning with salt and pepper.

4. Return it all to the casserole dish and cook in the preheated oven for 1½–2 hours. If the lid does not fit tight, put some aluminum foil underneath it. Watch that the contents do not dry out; if it looks in danger of doing so, add a little extra stock or water.

5. When the pheasant is almost done (that is, the legs are beginning to fall away), add the mushrooms. Of course, if you prefer, you could fry them lightly and put them in at the beginning. It is just a matter of how you like them.

6. When everything is done, if you had to add extra liquid during cooking, you may find there is too much in the pan and the gravy looks a bit thin. If that is the case, drain it off into a saucepan and return the casserole to the oven to keep warm, adding the plates and a serving dish too. Bring the liquid to a boil and sprinkle in a bit of flour while whisking or stirring with a wooden spoon until it begins to thicken. At the same time add the redcurrant jelly, and it should thicken up nicely.

7. Put the pheasant on a warmed serving dish, pour the gravy over it, and serve with your chosen vegetables.

Pheasant with Pigs' Trotters

As far as I know it was Joyce Molyneux of the Carved Angel restaurant in Dartmouth in the United Kingdom who first had the brilliant idea of using the wonderful gelatin and flavor of pigs' trotters to balance the leanness of the meat of the pheasant—sheer culinary genius. This is my version of the trotter and brandy–enhanced casserole. The trotters take 2 hours and should be cooked before the pheasant goes into the oven. Serve with mashed rutabagas, mashed potatoes (and celeriac if you like it), or mashed or roast parsnips.

For the Trotters

2 pigs' trotters

1¼ cup white wine

1 carrot, sliced

1 medium onion, sliced

1 stalk celery or ½ fennel bulb, sliced

1 bay leaf

2 sprigs thyme

3–4 cloves garlic, or to taste

For the Pheasant

1 tablespoon oil or butter

1 good, fat, well-hung pheasant

12 shallots or small onions about the size of shallots

1 4-ounce piece fat belly of pork or unsmoked bacon, cut into ½-inch cubes

2 tablespoons brandy, divided

2 cups stock (best to use the stock from cooking the trotters)

1 cup red wine

12 small mushrooms

1 bouquet garni (see page xvii)

1. Preheat the oven to 325°F. Tidy up the trotters if your butcher did not do so. The hairs are best singed, and a pair of good kitchen scissors should remove the toenails and any other loose bits.

2. Put everything to make the trotters into a lidded casserole dish (preferably Le Creuset) with 1¼ cups water and bring to a boil. This usually brings up a scum, which is best removed. Then put on the lid and cook in the pre-heated oven for about 2 hours or until it is tender, keeping an eye on it to make sure it does not dry out. Add more hot water if necessary.

3. To cook the pheasant, heat the oil or melt the butter in a stainless steel frying pan and brown the pheasant all over. Remove with a slotted spoon and keep warm in a large Pyrex (or similar) dish in the oven with the cooked trotters.

4. Brown the shallots or onions and the pork belly or bacon cubes in the frying pan until the shallots turn soft and golden.

5. Return the pheasant to the pan and, when all is nicely hot, pour in 1½ tablespoons of the brandy. Warm the remainder in the spoon using a match, and when all the fumes have subsided, return the pheasant, onions, and pork or bacon to the Pyrex dish. Remove the trotters from the oven and add them to the pheasant dish.

6. Strain the stock and pour it into the frying pan. Add the red wine, scraping up all the tasty bits stuck on the bottom of the pan, and bring it all to a boil.

7. Now get everything—the bird, the trotters, and the sauce—back into the casserole dish, adding the mushrooms and bouquet garni. If you like (and my wife does), you can also add the vegetables used with the trotters to make the stock. Put the lid on and cook in the oven for 1½ hours—or more if the pheasant needs it.

8. When the pheasant is ready, put it and the trotters onto a warm dish, surrounded by the shallots and mushrooms, and serve.

Pheasant with Brown Rice

This is one of the best complete meals that can be prepared, put in the oven, cleaned up, and almost forgotten until it comes out to the table. It is based on those chicken dishes you find from Greece and Spain and, as ever, you can adjust the ingredients to suit yourself. But do stick quite rigidly to the quantities of rice and liquids. I tend to measure rice by volume rather than weight, and you will need twice the volume of liquid (stock and white wine) as rice.

I prefer to do the frying bit of this recipe in my favorite deep, double-handled, stainless steel frying pan, and then I transfer everything to a brown pottery casserole dish that looks good on the table and holds heat better than steel, although I sometimes put the steel pan into the oven if I am in a hurry. Alternatively, you can do everything in a lidded casserole dish (preferably Le Creuset). If you have a gas stove you may prefer to let it all simmer there rather than use the oven, but I think electric stove tops (however good) are not suitable for long simmering.

3 tablespoons olive oil

1 good, fat, well-hung pleasant, jointed into 4 pieces (see page xiv)

1 medium Spanish or 2 regular onions, thickly sliced

2 red peppers or Romano peppers, deseeded, halved, and cut into ½-inch-wide strips

2 garlic cloves, to taste, crushed or chopped

1 cup brown rice (preferably basmati, which cooks more quickly)

1 cup game bird stock (see page xvi), chicken stock, or dry white wine

2 tablespoons tomato purée

2 tomatoes, chopped (or use sun-dried tomatoes in oil)

Salt and freshly ground black pepper

1 teaspoon chopped thyme

1 teaspoon chopped tarragon

½ teaspoon chopped rosemary

1. Preheat the oven to 350°F.

2. Heat the oil in a large frying pan and fry the pheasant pieces briefly—just so there's a gentle brown on both sides—then pop them into a casserole dish, put the lid on, and keep them warm in the oven.

3. Next, fry the onion and peppers, and when they begin to look cooked (after 4–5 minutes), add the garlic (and chorizo if you are using it). Stir in the rice with a wooden spoon to take up the remaining oil, just as you would for a risotto, then pour in the liquid—wine or stock—add the tomato purée and tomatoes and season with salt and pepper. Bring it all just to a boil, then simmer for a few minutes.

4. Now remove the pheasant from the casserole dish and transfer to a plate or dish. Put the rice mixture and liquid into the casserole, put the pheasant on top, add the herbs, and put the lid on. (If you are going for an Iberian style, add olives and orange pieces on top.) Cook in the oven for about 1 hour, but check after 45 minutes to make sure it is not drying out. If it is, add some water or wine. The cooking time is really more dependent on the rice than the pheasant: It needs to be soft but not mushy.

If you want a real Spanish flavor, you can add some slices of Spanish chorizo sausage, about 4 ounces— but don't forget to skin them—halved black olives, and a sliced orange.

Pheasant Breasts with Beets, Potatoes & Parsnips

You may have bought pheasant breasts on their own, or used the legs grilled, deviled, or as a starter or snack. In any case, for this recipe you will need two breasts each or three for larger appetites.

I think the beet is a much abused and underrated vegetable that in my childhood was always served swimming in vinegar to accompany cold meat and salad, or to eke out the cheese ration in sandwiches. Eaten young, just simply boiled or as one of a tray of mixed roasted vegetables, they are terrific—and they add color to a dish that would otherwise look a bit pallid. Just remember to break off rather than cut the leaves, leave on the root during cooking, and do not cut the beet in any way or it will bleed and lose color. This recipe serves 2–3 people.

2 or 3 small (but not button-size) beets, leaves broken off and root intact

1½ pounds potatoes, cut into chunks

8 ounces parsnips, cut into chunks

Salt

1 good-size tart apple, peeled, cored, and cut into chunks

1 tablespoon butter

1 tablespoon heavy cream or crème fraîche

Lots of chopped parsley or snipped chives—1½ tablespoons in all

6 pheasant breasts

2 teaspoons olive oil

1 glass white wine

¾ cup game bird stock (see page xvi) or chicken stock

2 teaspoons white flour

Mixed root vegetable crisps, for serving (optional)

1. It is best to start with the vegetables. The beets need cooking for around 60 minutes or more. Bring them to a boil, then cover and simmer until tender. Meanwhile, boil the potatoes and parsnips separately until tender (15–20 minutes). They will benefit from a pinch—but only a pinch—of salt. Soften the apple by popping it in with the parsnips or potatoes for a few minutes at the end of the cooking time.

2. Preheat the oven to a low setting for keeping plates, food, and so on warm. Once the potatoes and parsnips are cooked and the apple softened, drain them all, mix them in a saucepan, and let them dry off over a low heat. Then mash as you would plain potatoes with half of the butter, plus the cream and the parsley or chives. Transfer to a lidded serving dish and keep warm in the oven or over low heat—but do not let dry out. Drain the beets, cut into thick slices, and then put them in the warm oven too.

3. Now turn to the pheasant. Fry the breasts in a stainless steel pan in the olive oil until brown on both sides—it should take only a couple of minutes. Pour in the wine, bring briefly to a boil, and reduce by about a half. Add the stock and turn down to a brisk simmer until the breasts are cooked. (If they have come from a good young bird, this should take about 5 minutes.) Meanwhile, mix the remaining butter with the flour to make a beurre manié and keep to one side. When the breasts are done, transfer them to a dish and keep them warm in the oven with the vegetables.

4. Now raise the heat under the frying pan containing the meat juices and stock and, little by little, add the beurre manié, stirring with a wooden spoon as you do so, until it thickens and comes to a boil. Bring out the dish with the mashed potatoes and parsnips and arrange the pheasant breasts and beet slices on top, add the sauce, and serve. For a bit of extra show, it is quite nice to decorate the dish with some of those good mixed root vegetable crisps you find in the better places—like my village shop and better supermarkets.

Pheasant Breasts with Crème Fraîche

This is a simple fried breast recipe. One breast per person may be enough for light eaters, but those with better appetites would need both breasts of the average hen bird. Alternatively you could serve a leg and a breast for each person.

The amount of paprika is not a misprint—I do mean one tablespoon. The caraway seeds are not absolutely essential, but they do add something to the sauce, so they are worth trying. Serve this dish with your favorite potatoes and vegetables. Serves 2.

> 2 pheasant breasts and 2 legs
>
> 2 tablespoons olive oil or 1 tablespoon butter
>
> Roughly 1¼ cup crème fraîche
>
> 1 tablespoon paprika
>
> 1 tablespoon caraway seeds
>
> Some chopped parsley for garnish

Fry the pheasant pieces gently in the oil or butter in a stainless steel frying pan. The breasts will need about 5 minutes a side—the legs (if you are using them) will need more like 7 ½–8 minutes, so start them first. When they are done, add the crème fraîche, then stir in the paprika with a wooden spoon, and let the mixture simmer gently—do not let it boil or it will separate—for about 7–10 minutes. At the end add the caraway seeds, garnish with parsley, and serve. It really could hardly be simpler.

Deviled Pheasant (or Partridge)

We started by deviling the leftover turkey many, many years ago, then found a recipe for deviling the brown meat separately and serving it with the white meat in a cream sauce in Jane Grigson's great 1979 book *English Food*. It has changed a bit over the years in our kitchen, but not too much for the worse I hope. Here it has been adapted for pheasant or partridge, which is especially useful if, toward the end of the season, the children are starting to say, "Not pheasant again!"

These quantities are enough for a light supper dish. We like this with one (or two) chilled or frozen ready-to-cook garlic-butter baguettes, available, of course, from all good supermarkets. Remember they take about 20 minutes to cook.

1 cold roast or simply casseroled pheasant (or 2 partridges)

2 teaspoons chopped parsley

2 teaspoons chopped basil

For the Devil Sauce

2 tablespoons mango chutney (preferably Green Label)

1 tablespoon Worcestershire sauce

1 tablespoon Dijon mustard

2 teaspoons dry mustard powder

¼ teaspoon cayenne pepper

1 tablespoon olive oil

½ tablespoon butter

For the Cream Sauce

3 tablespoons butter

1 cup heavy cream

Juice of ½ lemon

Salt and freshly ground black pepper

1. Dismember the bird(s), cutting the brown meat off the legs, thighs, and wings, and cutting off and shredding the breast meat. Keep the 2 meats separate and put aside in the fridge.

2. Combine all the ingredients for the devil sauce in a bowl and mix thoroughly, making sure the lumpy bits of the chutney are mulched well into the mixture. Immerse the brown meat in the sauce and let it marinate for 3 or 4 hours in the fridge if you can.

3. When you are ready to cook, line the grill pan with aluminum foil, distribute the brown meat onto the rack with as much sauce on it as you can, and put under a really hot grill to brown and lightly crispen.

4. Meanwhile, make the cream sauce. Melt the butter in a large stainless steel pan, add the cream, and let it come almost to a boil while you keep stirring it with a wooden spoon to help it to thicken. Add the white meat and make sure it is all hot. Add the lemon juice, salt, and pepper.

5. Meanwhile, heat a serving dish and plates. Now put the deviled meat at one end of the serving dish and the white at the other, sprinkle with the herbs to give it a nice brown, white, and green color to it all.

Highland Pheasant

Not only are Scottish grouse rightly famed for their quality, but the pheasants from up there are pretty good too. This recipe gives a Scottish flavor and makes an enjoyable light supper or lunch dish.

    4 pheasant breasts

    1 haggis

    1 cup ready-to-eat dried apricots, finely chopped

    3 tablespoons whiskey, divided

    12 dry-cured streaky bacon slices

    Olive oil for drizzling

    ½ cup game bird stock (see page xvi) or chicken stock

    2 teaspoons cornstarch

    ½ cup heavy cream

    1 tablespoon chopped parsley

1. Preheat the oven to 350°F.

2. The easiest way to flatten the pheasant breasts is to put them between sheets of plastic wrap on a wooden board and bash them with a wooden rolling pin.

3. Crumble the haggis into a bowl, mix in the chopped apricots, and pour 1 tablespoon of the whiskey over it. Let it infuse for a few minutes. Divide this mixture into 4 portions and press into patties. Fold the pheasant breasts around these patties and wrap each with 3 slices of bacon. Cocktail sticks may be useful to keep them together. Put them on a baking sheet (preferably nonstick), drizzle with oil, and cook for 45–55 minutes.

4. While the haggis-pheasant patties are cooking, prepare the sauce. Gently heat the stock while stirring in the cornstarch with a wooden spoon, a bit at a time to avoid any lumps. Add the remaining whiskey, then let it all simmer for about 5 minutes. Gradually pour in the cream and let it all warm through. Add the chopped parsley.

5. Transfer the patties to a serving tray and spoon the sauce over them.

Pheasant Pâté

This recipe is from Game to Eat—the organization founded by the Country-side Alliance to promote the eating of game. I found it very straightforward.

> 8 ounces dry-cured streaky bacon slices, divided
>
> 12 ounces minced pheasant and 1 pheasant breast, diced
>
> 1½ pounds fat belly of pork
>
> 2 tablespoons brandy
>
> 1 garlic clove, crushed
>
> 6–8 juniper berries, chopped
>
> 2 tablespoons chopped rosemary
>
> 2 tablespoons chopped thyme
>
> Small bunch coriander, chopped
>
> A few bay leaves for decoration

1. Chop half the bacon into ¼-inch squares and mix in a bowl with the rest of the ingredients (except the other half of the bacon slices and bay leaves). Leave for an hour or so to combine the flavors thoroughly.

2. Preheat the oven to 300°F.

3. Put the ingredients into a terrine dish (preferably Le Creuset) and smooth the top. (If you do not have this dish, use an ovenproof baking dish of roughly the same dimensions, but go out tomorrow and buy one.) Lay the remaining streaky slices diagonally over the top. Decorate with the bay leaves, put the dish into a roasting pan of hot water so it comes halfway up the sides, and cook for 2–2 ½ hours with the lid on the terrine or a cover of extra thick (or doubled) aluminum foil over the top. You will know it is cooked when the pâté has shrunk away from the sides of the pan and the juices run clear if you stick it with a skewer.

4. When the pâté is done, remove it from the oven and squeeze it down with a similar-size dish or even a piece of flat, smooth wood with something heavy (packages of sugar, cans of something, or a brick wrapped in foil.) When it is cool, put it in the fridge for a few hours—or overnight—before shaking the pâté out and serving.

PARTRIDGE

[Phasianidae family]

*Despite quite colorful plumage partridges
are remarkably difficult to spot on the ground.
They fly low and, because they are
smaller than pheasants, they look to be
(but are not) a lot faster.*

You should find partridges in the shops, ready to cook. Like pheasants, they need to have been hung for six to seven days. A single bird is plenty enough for one person or would stretch to a light meal for two. Partridges casserole well and are easier and quicker to roast than pheasants. They also have a more delicate flavor than pheasants; so much so that one's first thought is often simply to roast them. However, partridge hot pots or casseroles—particularly with lentils and/or cabbage—certainly reward the extra time and trouble in preparation.

Partridge with Pears & Blue Cheese

This is my version of a recipe suggested by Game To Eat, a campaign that exists to promote the game meat industry. The recipe rests on the sound idea that since both partridges and cheese go well with pears, it's a good idea to put them together.

As to vegetables, you cannot go wrong with either baby new potatoes or crispy baked potatoes and whatever vegetables look good at the store or farmers' market. Mashed parsnips, or, if you had room in the oven, roasted parsnips and broad beans are ideal. You might also serve sliced roasted potatoes (see pages 11–12).

> 1 partridge per person
>
> 1 tablespoon butter, softened
>
> 2 streaky bacon slices per bird
>
> 1 pear per bird if small or ½ pear per bird if large, divided

> **The Remaining Ingredients Are Sufficient for 4 Birds**
>
> Vegetables for gravy—small onions or shallots, a carrot, a celery stalk
>
> 1 glass red wine
>
> A little white flour for thickening
>
> Chicken stock cube (optional)
>
> 4 ounces blue cheese, cut thinly into shavings

1. Preheat the oven to 400°F.

2. Tidy up the birds, trimming off the ends of the wings and plucking off any feathers. Rub a little of the butter around the insides and outsides of the birds and cover the legs and breasts with the bacon (use cocktail sticks to keep in place). Stuff the birds with a piece of pear—probably about a quarter will be enough.

3. Put the onions or shallots, carrot, and celery pieces in a roasting pan with about ½ cup boiling water—but make sure there is enough to cover the floor of the pan (the water needs to be boiling or it will take ages to get hot in the oven). Put a roasting rack in the pan and place the birds on the rack. Cover the pan with aluminum foil and put it into the oven for 30 minutes. (Yes, it is longer than for simple roast partridge, but the temperature is lower and they are under foil.)

4. While the birds are cooking, slice the rest of the pears in roundels or wagon wheels and remove the cores. Melt the rest of the butter in an oven dish. Turn the slices of pear in the melted butter and put them into the oven with the birds for the last 10 minutes of their cooking time.

5. After 30 minutes, remove the foil from the birds to let them and the bacon get crisp for another 10 minutes. A good way to do this is to put the birds on their rack in another pan and return them to the oven. You can then remove the vegetables from the first pan (if you like, save them in the warming oven with the plates) and bring the juices in the pan to a boil over a hot plate or on the stove top, add the red wine, and thicken with flour (and a stock cube, if you like). Use a wooden spoon to scrape all the bits off the bottom, and if you get it right this will also clean the pan!

6. Cooking times vary with the birds, your oven, and your taste. Serve the partridges and the bacon (if crisp enough, broken up) with the thickened sauce and the pears with blue cheese shavings on top.

Roast Partridge

This really could not be easier. It's best to keep it simple, and I would serve the bird and roasted potatoes with broccoli (but that's because I like roasted potatoes and broccoli), and I would not bother with bread sauce (because I think it is boring), but I give a recipe for it anyway.

Depending on the size of the potatoes, you will probably need to start cooking them in the roasting pan before the birds go in the oven on the rack over them. However, small new potatoes seem to be available throughout the winter these days, and they are ideal, as they take only about 20 minutes and so can go in at the same time as the birds.

As ever, timing is the tricky thing in this recipe, but if you make sure the gravy and bread sauce are done a little ahead of the birds, and that the broccoli is finishing cooking as the birds come out of the oven (cold broccoli is awful), all will be well.

> 4 partridges, wings clipped off and reserved for the stock
>
> A knob of butter, softened
>
> 2 large pears, halved, or 4 small pears
>
> 2 streaky bacon slices or 8 back slices
>
> Potatoes, for roasting

For the Gravy

Partridge wings and giblets (if you have them)

1 small onion, sliced

1 carrot, chopped

1 stalk celery, chopped

1 bay leaf

Thyme, parsley, oregano, or other spices, but not anything as strong as rosemary

1 glass white wine

A little white flour for thickening

Salt and freshly ground black pepper

Chicken stock cube (optional)

1 heaping teaspoon redcurrant jelly (optional)

1 glass red wine

For the Bread Sauce

4 ounces day-old white bread, thickly sliced then broken into bits

1¼ cups milk

1 small onion, halved

3 black peppercorns

2 cloves (if you like them)

1 bay leaf

1 tablespoon butter

Salt and freshly ground black pepper

1. To make the stock for the gravy, put the wings, giblets (if you have them), onion, carrot, celery, herbs, white wine, and about 1¼ cups water into a saucepan. Bring to a boil, then reduce to a simmer for 30 minutes.

2. While the stock simmers, put all the ingredients for the bread sauce, except for the butter, salt, and pepper, in a pan and leave to soak for about half an hour.

3. While the stock is simmering and the bread sauce ingredients are soaking, rub butter over the birds inside and out. Stuff each bird with a whole or half pear, depending on size. Cover with the bacon slices, using cocktail sticks to keep them in place.

4. Preheat the oven to 450°F.

5. Put the new potatoes in a roasting pan and put a roasting rack on top. Cook in the oven for 10 minutes, then place the birds on the rack and cook for another 20 minutes.

6. While the birds are cooking, warm the bread sauce ingredients, add the butter, and let it all thicken over very low heat, stirring occasionally with a wooden spoon, for about 15 minutes. Season with salt and pepper to give it some taste. Take out the onion, bay leaf, peppercorns, and cloves (if you used them) and transfer the sauce to a dish in the warm oven.

7. Sieve the stock into a pan and bring to a bubble, then thicken by sprinkling with a bit of flour and stirring with a wooden spoon. Season with salt and pepper to taste. If it looks thin (and tastes thin), add the stock cube or red-currant jelly, if using. As it thickens, add the red wine. Pour the sauce into a serving pitcher and place in the warm oven with the plates.

8. Remove the bacon from the birds after about 15 minutes if it is looking crisp, and let the birds brown for the final 5 minutes, but be quick about it and do not let the oven temperature fall. If you can resist the temptation to eat it on the spot, put that, too, into the warm oven until ready to serve.

Partridge Hot Pot

A hot pot of any kind is a wonderful dish on cold wet days. Substituting partridge for lamb gives it something extra for a family lunch or a smart dinner party. Use wine with the stock if you are entertaining, but cider if it's just the family. This recipe serves 4 hearty appetites.

4 partridges

2 pounds potatoes, cut into ¼-inch-thick slices

2 tablespoons olive oil

1 tablespoon butter

2–3 stalks celery, thinly sliced

2–3 leeks, thinly sliced

1¼ cups game bird or chicken stock (see page xvi)

1 large glass dry white wine or dry cider

1 heaping tablespoon white flour

1 teaspoon brown sugar (optional)

Salt and freshly ground black pepper to taste

1 teaspoon chopped thyme

1. Make sure the partridges are tidy. Remove the wings for the stock if there is not much to them. Preheat the oven to 325°F.

2. Put the potato slices into a pan of cold water and bring to a boil for a minute or so. Drain and put aside.

3. Heat the olive oil in a large stainless steel pan and fry the birds for about 10 minutes to brown on all sides. Then remove them to an ovenproof dish and keep hot in the oven.

4. Add as much of the butter as you need to the oil and juices in the stainless steel pan and fry the sliced celery and leeks until they soften and turn golden. Add the stock and wine or cider and bring to a bubble, adding the flour a little at a time to thicken; stir the mixture with a wooden spoon and use a stainless steel spatula to scrape all the bits off the bottom. Once that is done, you can, if you wish, sweeten with a little brown sugar and add salt and pepper to taste.

5. Put the birds along with the stock and leeks and celery in a casserole dish and sprinkle with the thyme. Dot the top with potato slices and put the casserole (without a lid) in the oven for about 1½ hours. By then the partridge should be tender and the potatoes soft with golden brown crispy edges.

Partridge with Dhal

By common consent, partridge and lentils go well together, and there are many good recipes for the combination. Remember that the dhal will take a while to prepare and cook, and it should be ready to go into the oven with the partridges.

2 tablespoons olive oil

1 tablespoon butter

4 partridges

4 ounces fat belly of pork or unsmoked bacon, cubed if 1 piece or sliced if thick

1 medium onion, finely chopped

1 large glass dry white wine

2 cups stock

For the Dhal

8 ounces lentils (the large green ones are best), soaked in water for at least 1 hour but preferably overnight

½ teaspoon ground turmeric

2 tablespoons chopped coriander

Salt

2 medium onions, chopped

1 garlic clove, crushed

1–2 tablespoons olive oil or ½ tablespoon butter or cooking fat

1 8-ounce can chopped tomatoes or 3–4 fresh tomatoes, skinned

1. To make the dhal, drain the lentils, put them into 4 cups of boiling water; add the turmeric, coriander, and a little salt; and then let them simmer.

2. In the meantime, fry the chopped onions and garlic in the oil, butter, or cooking fat, add the tomatoes and fry gently until all are soft. Then add this mixture to the lentils and simmer for 30 minutes.

3. Preheat the oven to 325°F. Heat the oil and butter in a large stainless steel pan and fry the partridges on all sides to get them nicely browned. Remove to a lidded casserole (ideally a large Le Creuset).

4. In the remaining fat (add a little more if need be), fry the pork belly or bacon until the juices flow, then add the onion and fry until tender and golden. Return the partridges to the pan, add the wine, and bring to a boil. Add the stock and turn down to a simmer, making sure to scrape off all the bits stuck to the bottom of the pan and stir them into the stock with a wooden spoon.

5. Add the dhal to the casserole dish, burying the partridges in it. Add the stock, put the lid on the casserole dish, and put it all into the oven. As always, cooking time depends on the birds. Have a time of about 45 minutes in mind—but don't eat by the clock. Cook until the birds are tender.

I have left out the chile that would
go into a dhal to accompany a curried bird.

Partridge Risotto

I love risottos. Of course you must have good Arborio rice—do not bother to try to make a risotto with anything else—but the variety of meat, fish, or vegetables you can use is enormous. My favorites are chicken liver or, in the spring, really young, fresh broad beans and peas or seafood—particularly shrimp, squid, and mussels—or mushrooms. And, of course, you can use partridge for something even more substantial. This is my version of a Game to Eat recipe. The basic recipe is the same for all risottos, but if you do try the chicken livers, do not overcook them. Chop them into bite-size pieces, fry very lightly at the beginning, and then remove and reserve them in a warm place and add right at the end. If you overcook them, they will be like little leather buttons.

The Game to Eat recipe suggests reserving the breasts, slicing them, and adding them to the risotto when it is well cooked, together with a little arugula and baby spinach as a garnish. I am not much on garnishes, but you may like it.

2 partridges

4 cups hot chicken or partridge stock (see page xvi)

1 bay leaf

A sprinkle of thyme

6 black peppercorns

2 tablespoons olive oil

1 medium onion, finely chopped

1 garlic clove, crushed

1½ cups Arborio rice

1 large glass dry white wine

1 tablespoon butter (optional)

1 tablespoon Parmesan cheese shavings

2 teaspoons chopped parsley

Salt

1. Start by removing the legs and breasts from the birds. Put the carcasses into the stock in a large saucepan, with the bay leaf, thyme, and peppercorns. Bring to a boil, simmer for 30 minutes, then drain off the stock and keep it warm. Take the meat off the legs and chop it quite small. Slice the breasts and chop them too, but not quite so small, and keep them separate.

2. Heat the olive oil in a fairly deep, heavy pan and gently fry the onions and garlic to a light color. Add the rice and stir with a wooden spoon to ensure all of it is coated with oil. Once the oil is all absorbed, add the white wine and, as it boils up, add a ladle of warm stock. Turn down the heat a little but keep the stock just bubbling, and stir gently with a wooden spoon. As the stock gets absorbed, add another ladle of stock, repeating the process until you find that quite suddenly the grains of rice puff up and become softened. Do not overdo it and produce a glutinous mess. If you run out of stock, use a little warm water.

3. While the rice is cooking, gently fry the chopped-up meat in the butter, giving the leg meat a minute or two start over the breast. When the rice is almost done, add the meat to it. Make sure it is well mixed and cooked through. Some people add a little butter or even a spoonful of cream. I don't, but try it for yourself.

4. Sprinkle on the Parmesan and parsley and salt if desired. Serve straight from the pan.

Partridge Paella

As with risotto, this basic recipe can be used with rabbit or chicken as well as seafood—especially prawns, squid, clams, and mussels. (The Spanish mix meat and fish, so you can, too.) I do not add much—if any—salt, but that is a matter of taste. I like the color and flavor of the saffron, but you may prefer turmeric.

2 partridges, each jointed into 4 pieces, removing the breasts and
    saving the carcass for the stock

2 tablespoons olive oil

6 ounces chorizo sausage, skinned and sliced

1 medium onion, chopped

2 tomatoes, peeled and chopped

1½ cups paella rice

2 tablespoons peas (optional)

½ teaspoon paprika

½ teaspoon powdered saffron

For the Stock

1 bay leaf

1–2 sprigs thyme

6 black peppercorns

Celery (optional)

Salt and freshly ground black pepper

1. Put the carcasses into 5 cups of water with the stock ingredients and bring up to a boil. Turn down to simmer for 30 minutes, then drain off the stock and keep it warm on the stove.

2. Heat the oil in a heavy deep pan (a stainless steel one is ideal) and fry the partridge meat and sliced chorizo sausage. I leave the legs whole but slice each breast into at least 2 slices. When these are all cooked, remove and keep warm.

3. Now fry the onions and chopped tomatoes in the same pan. Once the onion is golden, add the rice and let it absorb any oil left in the pan (just as you would for a risotto), but then add all the stock, bring briefly to a boil, turn down to simmer, add the partridge meat and sausage, and leave to simmer for 10 minutes or so before adding the peas (if you are using them), paprika, and saffron. The rice should be cooked in another 5–10 minutes, but that is very variable, depending on the rice. If the stock has all been absorbed before the rice is done (al dente but not soggy), add a little more hot water. If the rice is done before all the stock has been absorbed just turn up the heat a little to evaporate it.

4. Serve directly from the pan.

Partridge Tagine with Olives & Lemon

They tell me that a tagine is actually a traditional North African conical cooking pot, rather than the dish itself. Rather like a casserole, I suppose. Usually over here it seems to be a spicy meat dish, often with apricots. Debby Mason brought this recipe back from Morocco. Serve with boiled rice or couscous. Serves 6.

2 tablespoons olive oil

6 partridges

3 medium onions, sliced

1 good pinch saffron threads

1 tablespoon chopped garlic

1 teaspoon ground cumin

1 teaspoon ground ginger

1 teaspoon paprika

1 teaspoon turmeric

1 teaspoon ground cinnamon

2 cinnamon sticks

1 pinch cayenne pepper

2 cups game bird stock (see page xvi) or chicken stock

½ cup fresh lemon juice

1 large preserved lemon, pipped and sliced

¾ cup pitted green and black olives

1 small bunch flat-leaf parsley, chopped

1 small bunch coriander, chopped

Salt

1. Preheat the oven to 350°F.

2. Heat the oil in a large heavy casserole dish with a well-fitting lid and gently fry the partridges until browned on all sides, about 10 minutes in all. Remove and set them aside.

3. Fry the onions gently in the fat and oil left in the pan until soft and golden. Stir in the spices with a wooden spoon, mixing them well into the onions, and fry for another couple of minutes. Enjoy the wonderful smell of all that! Mason says it takes her back to Jemaa El Fna in Marrakesh, where the spice sellers rub shoulders with snake charmers, dodgy dentists, herbalists, gulli-gulli men, and acrobats.

4. Forgetting all that and returning to the kitchen, return the partridges to the casserole dish over medium-high heat, add the stock and lemon juice, bring to a boil, and then turn down to a slow simmer, with the lid partly on, for 20 minutes, giving it a stir now and again with a wooden spoon. Stir in the lemon slices and olives with a wooden spoon, put the lid on firmly, and put the dish in the oven for 20–30 minutes, or until the partridges are cooked through but still just pink.

5. Check the seasoning, sprinkle with chopped parsley and coriander. Add salt if desired, and serve.

WILD DUCK

[Anas platyrhynchos]

48 | Crumbed Roast Duck

50 | Roast or Grilled Duck Breasts with a Fruit Sauce

51 | Duck Leg Stew

"Damned silly bird the duck.
Too much for one
and not enough for two"

I DO NOT FIND THAT WILD DUCKS ARE THE EASIEST BIRDS to cook well. Unlike the domesticated puddle ducks, which are very fat, wild ducks are leaner and more muscular. I recollect one night when I was navigating a Second World War York freighter (which had wings and Merlin engines of a Lancaster bomber attached to a more capacious body) across the Sahara from Nigeria to Libya that we collided with an unfortunate duck coming the other way. The bird flew straight into the radiator of one of the four Merlin engines, which then overheated by the time we reached Tripoli. Even without the hazard of aircraft bumbling along through the night at 180 knots at 6,000 to 10,000 feet, that crossing must be quite a challenge to even a muscular duck.

These recipes are all based on mallard, which is really the only wild duck you are likely to find in the shop. I once used Mandarin ducks, which were shot in error from a flock of about twenty that were taken for very high mallard. If you are lucky enough to acquire any teal, they will look and cook very much like mallard.

If you are cooking wild duck whole (particularly roasting), the difficult part is to avoid either drying up the breasts or undercooking the legs. One answer is to cook them separately. Another is to coat them with a bread-crumb crust, and I give recipes for both options. The casserole or stew of the duck legs I find particularly good.

That said, there is one other difficulty with wild duck. As an aristocratic London clubman (I cannot remember who) said, "Damned silly bird the duck. Too much for one and not enough for two."

Crumbed Roast Duck

I recommend removing the legs from these ducks to make the duck stew on page 51, or indeed simply to fry with onion, herbs, and crushed garlic, to eat as an hors d'oeuvre. Of the options for roasting I prefer the crumb casing. Indeed I think casing almost any fowl or meat in a butter–herb–bread crumb coating adds something extra to the sight, smell, and taste of the dish. Some years ago I adapted this recipe from a favorite Sophie Grigson recipe for rack of lamb with an herb crust. Choose your fruit flavor. The most popular flavor is probably orange, but try others too, such as dried or fresh apricots or dates or quarters of apple. This recipe serves 4.

> 2 oranges
>
> 2 ducks, legs removed and reserved (see page 51)
>
> 2½ tablespoons butter, softened
>
> 5 ounces fresh white bread crumbs
>
> 1 garlic clove, crushed
>
> Herbs of your choice, lots of them, chopped
>
> Salt and freshly ground black pepper

1. Preheat the oven to 450°F.

2. Finely grate the zest of 1 of the oranges and squeeze the juice. Slice the second orange into rounds.

3. Butter the inside of the ducks with no more than ½ tablespoon of the butter and smear a little more on the outside of the birds. Put as many orange rounds (according to size) as seems sensible into the bird cavities. That is, you are not stuffing them—just adding flavor. If you prefer, use apricots, dates, or apples.

4. Soften the rest of the butter and work into the bread crumbs to get a sticky mixture together with the garlic and herbs. Add the orange zest and juice and season with salt and pepper. Plaster the birds with the crumb mixture, then put them on a roasting rack in a roasting pan and cook in the oven for 30 minutes or so until done with the breast still pink.

Roast or Grilled Duck Breasts with a Fruit Sauce

If you are cooking for four adults with light appetites—or serving this dish as a first course—one breast each would do nicely, but as a main course for healthy appetites, I would be tempted to do two breasts per person. You can make the sauce well ahead of time—but keep it warm until you are ready to use it. If you buy whole ducks, you will have the legs for a duck stew (see page 51) and the carcasses for stock.

>   1 pound black currants or ripe plums, halved and stoned
>
>   1 cinnamon stick
>
>   Glass dry white wine
>
>   1 tablespoon wine vinegar
>
>   Sugar to taste—preferably caster but granulated will do
>
>   Freshly ground black pepper
>
>   4 duck breasts
>
>   Olive oil for brushing
>
>   Salt

1. Put the black currants or plums, cinnamon stick, white wine, and wine vinegar into a saucepan. Let it come briefly to a boil, then turn down to just simmer gently until the fruit is really soft. Pour into a stainless steel sieve and push it through with a wooden spoon into the saucepan, add the sugar and heat until it dissolves into the fruit. Add black pepper to taste—I use quite a lot. Keep the sauce warm over a gentle heat while you cook the duck.

2. For roasting the duck, preheat the oven to 425°F. Brush the breasts with oil and lay them cut-side down on a roasting rack in a roasting pan. Put plenty of salt and pepper on the skin side and cook for 10 minutes if the breasts are on the thin side or a few minutes more to make sure they are cooked—but still just pink. Alternatively, grill under a very hot grill for 5 minutes a side, or a bit more if you like them well done.

3. When cooked, let the breasts rest for 1–2 minutes in a warming oven (if you don't have one, simply leave the oven door open) and then serve surrounded by sauce.

Duck Leg Stew

For every duck breast there is a duck leg and half a carcass for stock, and you can make this as simple or as exotic as you like. Use the legs to make a rather tasty stew or casserole. If you can't find the canned beans you want, use some well-soaked dry ones—or lentils—all available at good supermarkets. This recipe serves 4 as a first course or light lunch.

For the Stock

2 duck carcasses

6–8 peppercorns

1 stalk celery, chopped

1 bay leaf and some parsley and thyme to taste

1 onion, chopped, or 2 shallots, chopped in half

1 large or 2 small carrots, roughly chopped

For the Stew

4 duck legs

White flour, enough to cover the duck legs

½ tablespoon butter

4 ounces streaky bacon, chopped

2 shallots, chopped

2 carrots, chopped

1¼ cups red wine

Selection of herbs, such as thyme, parsley, marjoram

7 ounces canned chopped tomatoes

½ 14-ounce can (or a small can, if you can find it) flageolet or cannellini beans or lentils, drained and rinsed

Salt and freshly ground black pepper

1. To make the stock, put all the ingredients in a saucepan and cover with water. Bring to a boil, then simmer gently with the lid on for ½ hour, skimming off any scum with a slotted spoon at intervals. Allow to cool, then strain and measure out 2 cups. Freeze any surplus in ice-cube trays.

2. Preheat the oven to 325°F (if you plan to cook the stew on the stove, see below). Season the flour, then roll the duck legs in it. Melt the butter in a large stainless steel pan (with a lid if available) and briefly fry the legs and bacon, then put them aside.

3. Fry the shallots and carrots in the remaining fat. Add the wine, reserved stock, herbs, tomatoes, and beans. Return the duck legs and bacon bits to the pan. Bring it all to a boil, season to taste with salt and pepper, then reduce to a slow simmer. If you have used a deep pan with a lid, you can either leave it to simmer on the stove for 45 minutes or put it all into a casserole dish and heat it in the oven.

GROUSE

[Lagopus lagopus]

*The grouse season opens on
August 12—the Glorious Twelfth!*

THE BLACK GROUSE (*Tetrao tetrix*) is far less common than the
red. It is both bigger and heavier, but, like the red, has been the
victim of human pressures on its habitat of ancient pinewoods.
They are beautifully camouflaged and fly fast and low. They are
challenging birds to shoot and, of course, excellent to eat.

Roast Grouse

There is really only one way to cook grouse. That is to simply roast it and then eat it either hot or cold. Jane Grigson suggests putting fruit inside the bird—bananas, raspberries, cranberries or grapes. Sophie is all for serving them with bread sauce (something for which I have never found much use at all). For my part, I think it best to keep it really simple—especially as I usually finish up with the carcass in my fingers.

You may wish to have some vegetables, although they can just get in the way of unrestrained grouse guzzling. Probably the best accompaniment would be braised red cabbage.

A little lemon juice

1 tablespoon butter, softened

4 grouse

8 or 12 fat belly of pork or unsmoked bacon slices

2 tablespoons olive oil

4 thick slices good white bread

2 tablespoons bread crumbs per bird

Watercress for garnish

Cranberry, rowan, or redcurrant jelly, to serve

1. Preheat the oven to 375°F.

2. Add a drop or two (no more) of lemon juice to the softened butter and smear it around the inside of each bird. Cover the birds with the pork belly or bacon slices, using 2 or 3 per bird—cocktail sticks help keep them in place.

3. Put the birds on a roasting rack in a roasting pan and roast for 25–35 minutes, then remove the pork belly or bacon and put the birds back in the oven to brown for another 10 minutes. (If you prefer to roast hotter and quicker, then cook at 425°F for 25 minutes.)

4. If you have the grouse livers, you can let them cook inside the birds and then remove them. That can be a lot of work, however, and it can be easier simply to take them out before you cook the bird and fry them very quickly before you fry the bread.

5. While the birds are finishing browning, heat the olive oil in a large frying pan and fry the bread to use as croutons. (You may need to do this in batches.) Then just brown the bread crumbs in the hot oil.

6. Remove the birds from the oven. Set them on the croutons with the livers softened to a paste. Garnish with watercress, sprinkle with the fried bread crumbs, and serve with the cranberry, rowan, or redcurrant jelly.

WOOD PIGEON

[Columba palumbu]

*A beautiful bird,
but not in my garden
or in crops.*

THE MORE WE OBSERVE BIRDS, THE LESS APT THE PEJORATIVE expression "bird brain" seems to be. Wood pigeons are not easy to shoot in flight with a shotgun: They recognize people carrying guns and will often keep out of range. Even when the chance of a good overhead shot presents itself, the wary pigeon often seems to detect the flash of the gun and jinks like a bomber caught in the searchlights avoiding the flak. I never feel a day's shooting is quite complete without getting a wood pigeon.

They can be as much a pest in the garden (particularly the vegetable patch) as in a wheatfield, and I use a .22 compressed air rifle from the bedroom window—when I get the chance. All too often, however, the wary wood pigeon is up and away before I have unlatched, let alone opened, the window.

At a maximum weight of about 1¼ pounds (including a crop packed full of wheat or barley), there is not a lot to eat on a pigeon, but whether you just take the breasts and leave the rest for the local fox, or whether you use the whole bird, the wood pigeon is good food— although you need one per head.

Pigeon with Cabbage

Pigeon is not a delicate flavor, and because you can never be quite sure how old the birds are, slow cooking with cabbage brings out the best in them. I do not think this dish really needs other vegetables, but if you are feeding hungry teenagers, you can't go wrong with baked potatoes and steamed carrots.

4 pigeons

2–3 tablespoons olive oil

4 slices unsmoked fat bacon, chopped

2 medium onions, chopped

1 large red, green, or savoy (my favorite) cabbage—or better still, 2 small ones, cored and sliced thinly

2 tart apples, peeled, cored, and chopped

Salt and freshly ground black pepper

1 teaspoon chopped raisins (optional)

1 teaspoon soft brown sugar (optional)

½ cup red wine

½ cup game bird stock (see page xvi) or chicken stock

1. Preheat the oven to 325°F.

2. Remove the breasts, legs, and wings from the birds (reserve the carcasses for a stock or soup base), in a similar way to jointing a pheasant (see page xiv).

3. Heat the oil in a deep stainless steel pan. Start the bacon frying gently, then fry the pigeon pieces. Do not overdo them. When they are nicely browned, transfer them to a warm place.

4. Fry the onions in the remaining juices, then the cabbage, and then the apples, using the rest of the oil if the cabbage has absorbed all that is in the pan. Season with salt and pepper and add the raisins or sugar if you like a touch of sweetness.

5. You can either put the pigeon pieces on top of the cabbage mixture in the big stainless steel pan if it has a good lid, or put it all into an earthenware casserole dish with a tight-fitting lid. Add the red wine and stock and let it cook for at least 1½ hours.

Fried Pigeon Breasts

There are many good cooks, Clarissa Dickson Wright of Two Fat Ladies fame among them, who reckon you can simply fry pigeon breasts and serve them direct from the pan. Well, you can if you are satisfied that they come from a young pigeon. But every now and again you are bound to find you have something that is best to slip under the table to the dog.

Dickson suggests just rolling the breasts in flour seasoned with paprika, salt, pepper, and dry mustard powder and frying them in butter for 5 minutes a side. If they are young, that is fine, and if you like you could pour some thick cream into the pan as the breasts are almost done, add a drop of lemon juice, and serve on fresh hot toast, but check the bird's birth certificate first!

Casseroled Pigeon Breasts

For this recipe you use just the breasts (and make stock from the remaining carcasses), which makes the actual eating business rather simple, as opposed to picking up the bird and chewing it. As for vegetables, as always I would go for either baked potatoes or mashed and creamed potatoes with celeriac (see page xviii) or, in season, really new potatoes and whichever vegetables are seasonally at their best.

½ tablespoon butter

2 tablespoons olive oil

4 pigeons, either cooked whole or just the 8 breasts removed and cooked separately

12 small onions—the really little ones, the size of quails eggs—or shallots

8 ounces unsmoked back bacon slices

8 ounces mushrooms, the chestnut variety is ideal

Salt and freshly ground black pepper

½ cup pigeon or chicken stock

1 large glass red wine

2 tablespoons brandy

1. Preheat the oven to 325°F.

2. Heat the butter and oil in a large, deep, stainless steel frying pan and brown the birds or breasts, then remove them to a lidded casserole dish (preferably Le Creuset) with a slotted spoon.

3. Lightly brown the onions, bacon, and mushrooms. Place the onions and mushrooms around the birds or breasts and place the bacon over them; season with salt and pepper.

4. Bring the stock to a boil in the frying pan, scraping off the bottom any bits that may have stuck and incorporating them into the liquid. Add the wine then, as it all comes back to a boil, add the brandy and pour the liquid over the birds or breasts. Put on the lid and put the dish into the oven to cook. If the birds are young, this should take about 1 hour—but be prepared to give them another ½ hour if necessary. (You can use a fork to test it, or cut a bit off and try it.) Check after ½ hour to make sure that the meat is not drying out; add more stock if necessary.

Complete Pigeon Casserole

This is a good way to cook those pigeons that might be beyond their first flush of youth. I think it goes well with baked potatoes (but you'll need a double oven, as they really need to be cooked at 400°F), but mashed potatoes are good too, and carrots or broccoli add some extra color.

> 2 good-size pigeons, cut in half lengthwise using a pair of poultry scissors (see below)
>
> 1 tablespoon butter
>
> 8 ounces fat belly of pork (you can use bacon slices, but they won't be nearly as good), cut into ½-inch cubes
>
> 2–3 shallots or 1 medium onion, thinly sliced
>
> 1 large garlic clove, chopped
>
> 4 ounces mushrooms (preferably portobello, chestnut, or wild field mushrooms), sliced
>
> 1¼ cups dark ale or red wine
>
> 1¼ cup game bird stock (see page xvi) or chicken stock
>
> 1 bouquet garni (see page xvii)
>
> Salt and freshly ground black pepper

1. Preheat the oven to 350°F. Take poultry scissors and, starting from the back end of the bird, cut along the line of the breastbone right to the neck cavity. Then pull the two sides of the bird apart and sever along the line of the backbone into the 2 halves.

2. Melt the butter in an ovenproof casserole dish (I also use my favorite big stainless steel lidded pan) and fry the pork cubes and pigeon pieces. Once they are browned, set them aside on a plate and gently fry the shallots or onion with the garlic and mushrooms. Add the dark ale or wine, stock, and bouquet garni and bring to a boil for a moment while you scrape those good bits off the bottom of the pan.

3. Return the pigeons, put on a well-fitting lid, and cook in the oven for 1 hour or until the birds are tender. Add salt and pepper if desired.

Pigeon Breasts with Fruit Sauce

With every respect to Clarissa Dickson Wright, who likes pigeon breasts unadorned, I think they can be improved with a fruit sauce—and my favorite is a blackberry one.

On their own, as in this recipe, these pigeon breasts make an excellent quick brunch, but if served with winter vegetables such as carrots and potatoes mashed with celeriac or a summer salad of arugula, beet leaves, baby spinach, spring onions, tomatoes, and fresh boiled beets, they will make a main meal.

> 1–2 tablespoons olive oil
>
> 8 pigeon breasts
>
> **for the fruit sauce**
>
> 1¼ cup game bird stock (see page xvi) or chicken stock
>
> 2 tablespoons white wine vinegar or white wine
>
> 4 tablespoons redcurrant jelly
>
> A little white flour for thickening
>
> 8 ounces blackberries

1. Pour the olive oil onto a deep plate and quickly turn the pigeon breasts in it. Sear them on a hot griddle pan—Le Creuset, as always, is best—for about 2 minutes a side, then remove from the pan and reserve in a warm place covered with foil.

2. Add the stock and the wine vinegar or white wine to the pan, initially bringing the liquid to a boil to scrape up any juices and burnt bits from the pigeon breasts. Then, as it begins to reduce, lower the heat a little and add the redcurrant jelly, stirring it in with a wooden spoon to dissolve. Once it begins to thicken (and you can hasten that by adding some flour but only a little bit, not by spoonfuls), add the blackberries and let them cook until they are soft.

3. Slice the warm pigeon breasts, put them back on their warm dish, and pour the blackberry sauce over them.

WOODCOCK

[Scolopax rusticola]

*A beautiful bird—but don't let
my sentimentality put you off eating it.*

THE WOODCOCK IS A LITTLE SMALLER THAN A WOOD PIGEON. Living in woodlands, particularly those on boggy or soft soil, and being wonderfully camouflaged, woodcocks will scarcely be seen by town dwellers. Unless you almost tread on the bird, putting it up to flight, you could walk unknowingly past one. In flight it is made quite distinctive by the noisy beat of its broad wings, its swift flight through the trees, and, of course, its long, slightly curved back.

Woodcocks are good to eat, but I have to confess to a touch of sentimental weakness. In most places that I shoot there are not a lot of woodcocks, and they are such beautiful birds with such a graceful flight and half melancholy call, that I just cannot find the will to shoot them.

However, if you find it at the butcher's, or are given one, do not let my sentimentality keep you from eating it—I wouldn't. There is only one way to cook this bird—roast it—but let it hang for five to six days first.

Roast Woodcocks on Toast

A woodcock should be cooked whole—with the head on. Remove the crop and gizzard before cooking, but leave the trail (liver, heart, and intestines) where it is.

> 4 woodcocks
>
> 4 pieces of pork fat, enough to cover the birds
>
> Lemon juice to taste
>
> 4 teaspoons brandy
>
> Salt and freshly ground pepper
>
> 4 slices white bread

1. Preheat the oven to 450°F.
2. Cover each bird with a piece of pork fat and put them on a roasting rack in a roasting pan. They will be done in 18–20 minutes.
3. Take the birds out of the oven, remove each bird's trail, and in a small, warm saucepan, mash them and mix with a good squeeze of lemon juice, the brandy, and some salt and pepper.
4. Meanwhile, toast the bread. Spread the trail mixture on the toast, put a bird on top of each one, and eat while hot.

DEER

[Cervidae family]

The king of game.

I LOVE VENISON. DO NOT BE PUT OFF BY THOSE PEOPLE (generally who have never eaten it) who say it is too gamey. It is far more likely to be lacking flavor because it has not been hung long enough. Generally speaking it is cooked like beef (and to be really good beef should be hung for three to four weeks in a butcher's cool room). It is leaner than beef so needs even more care in cooking.

You can adapt the recipe for roasting a whole haunch in flour and water paste for any large joint. Otherwise (especially with small three- to five-pound roasting joints), it is wise to marinate overnight before cooking to prevent the meat from drying out.

Simple Roast Venison

A good butcher will be able to supply venison already boned and rolled for roasting. Remember: Venison is lean meat, so it is healthy eating but also needs careful cooking because of the lack of fat. I always recommend marinating the meat overnight. For a normal-size joint, I would make a half quantity of the marinade for the Roast Haunch of Venison on page 75.

It is also well worthwhile to lard the joint with thin strips of bacon fat known as lardoons and wrap it in a fatty piece of pork sink, if you can get it from your butcher.

Cook the joint at 350°F for 20 minutes per pound plus 20 minutes. Bigger joints need proportionally less time: Say 15 minutes per pound plus 15 minutes for a joint of 5 pounds. Do not overcook venison: Like good beef, if it is well hung it is best a little pink.

There will not be much in the pan from which to make gravy, so you might like a sauce. Venison goes with port wine, redcurrant jelly, orange or lemon, cinnamon, and allspice. Choose the ingredients to suit yourself, but Jane Grigson recommends Queen Victoria's favorite, which is very simple and is included below.

> 2 tablespoons port (which I thought too little)
>
> 1 cup redcurrant jelly (which I found too much)
>
> 1 small stick cinnamon
>
> Zest of 1 lemon

Place all the ingredients together in a pan, gently warm, and stir together with a wooden spoon.

Roast Haunch of Venison

The roast haunch of venison has been a classic English dish for the last thousand years at least. It was served, no doubt in style, in castles, great houses, and bishops' palaces and, in secret, in humble homes under threat of dire punishment for taking deer. Nowadays it is only the problem of finding a butcher who will sell you a haunch (and the cash to pay him) that need hold you back. The size will very greatly from the muntjac to the magnificent red, so you might have a very large, or quite small, haunch. That need not affect the marinade, but you might need more or less flour-and-water paste for the coating.

When I was a minister in Margaret Thatcher's government, ministers were, from time to time, offered a haunch from the deer culled in the Royal Parks, an offer I could not bring myself to refuse, even though the only place to hang it in our London home was the bathroom.

The haunch needs to be marinated for twenty-four hours before cooking. As for the vegetables, potatoes—new or mashed—creamed with celeriac, French beans or broad beans, all go well.

For the Marinade

2 cups red wine

2 tablespoons olive oil

4 tablespoons red wine vinegar

4 medium onions, sliced

2 stalks celery

2 large (or 4 small) carrots, sliced

1 bay leaf

12 black peppercorns

12 juniper berries

4 garlic cloves, crushed

1 teaspoon chopped thyme

Zest of ¼ orange

For the Venison

1 haunch venison, hung for 7–10 days

A knob of butter

4 ounces pork fat, cut into thin strips, known as lardoons

1 pound white flour, and a little more for the gravy

¼ cup suet

2 carrots, split lengthwise

1 onion, quartered (or several small shallots)

1 stalk celery, chopped

1. Put all the marinade ingredients in a large lidded container and mix together. Put the venison in the marinade, cover, and leave to marinate for 24 hours.

2. Preheat the oven to 325°F.

3. Remove the venison from the marinade (save the marinade for the gravy) and make sure it's well dried. Rub the butter into the meat. Using a larding needle, thread the lardoons of pork fat into the venison—or with a sharp knife, cut incisions and squeeze in the pieces of fat.

4. Put the flour and suet in a bowl, mix with enough water to make a really sticky paste with which to plaster the haunch, using your hands to do so (you may need more or less than this according to the size of your haunch). Cover the venison completely with the paste, sealing it inside. Then wrap it all in grease-proof paper and tie up with string.

5. Put the haunch on a roasting rack in a large roasting pan. Cover the bottom of the pan with boiling water and cook in the oven for 4–5 hours according to size. (A starting guess would be about 15 minutes per pound.) About halfway through the cooking time, by which time the juices should have dripped through the paste coating, put the vegetables under the rack, topping off the water if necessary.

6. Half an hour before the estimated cooking time, remove the venison from the oven and remove the paste coating. This will let you check with a carving fork to see how well done the meat is and give an idea of when to start the vegetables.

7. Venison needs to be served good and hot (or completely cold), so it is best at this stage to set the haunch on one side for 1–2 minutes, pour some boiling water into the roasting pan, put it over a high heat on the stove, scrape up all the burned bits, pour them into a saucepan, and then return the joint to the roasting pan and into the oven as quickly as possible to resume cooking. You can make the gravy in the saucepan, thicken up with flour and add some of the marinade for extra flavor and color.

Venison Steaks

Just like beefsteaks, venison steaks can be grilled, fried or, if the weather is right, barbecued. It is not a bad idea to tenderize and bring out the flavor of venison steaks by marinating them for at least two hours, preferably four hours.

4 venison steaks, whatever size you fancy

For the Marinade

½ cup red wine

1 tablespoon olive oil

1 small onion, chopped

2 garlic cloves, crushed

2 teaspoons English mustard

1 tablespoon brown sugar (if you like your barbecue marinated sweet)
   or a little chilli powder sprinkled on the steaks (if you like it hot)

1. Mix the marinade ingredients well, add the steaks, cover, and leave to marinate for 2–4 hours.

2. Drain the steaks well before cooking. If you are barbecuing them, you can use the marinade during cooking to prevent the outside from burning before the steak is done. Personally, I prefer to use a really heavy Le Creuset skillet in the comfort of my kitchen and to eat my steak slightly crispened on the outside and pink in the middle.

Minute Venison Fillet Steaks

I have borrowed this recipe from my friends in the Game to Eat campaign by the Countryside Alliance and the National Game Dealers' Association. If you use one of those splendid Le Creuset heavy skillets, you need not use the butter; just brush the pan and steaks with olive oil and keep the cholesterol down. This will go well with a mixed arugula, watercress, and baby spinach salad.

4 venison fillet steaks

For the Sauce

2 tablespoons port

8 ounces redcurrant jelly

2 teaspoons butter

1 tablespoon olive oil

Salt and freshly ground black pepper

4 ounces Somerset Brie

1. Gently warm the port in a small pan, dissolve the redcurrant jelly into it, and keep warm over a low heat.

2. If the steaks are thick, put them on a wooden board, cover with wax paper or plastic wrap, and bash them with a wooden rolling pin to reduce to about ¼-inch thickness to tenderize them.

3. Melt the butter in the oil in a heavy pan, season the steaks with salt and pepper to taste, and cook (but do not overcook!).

4. Serve with a slice of Brie on each steak (I think it best to put the Brie on the steak in the pan just before it is done) with a little of the port and redcurrant sauce.

Venison Casserole with Beer

It used to be that no one wanted shoulder of venison, but I fear the word has got out that like those less popular cuts of beef (my favorite is shin), it makes an excellent casserole or stew. There are as many recipes for venison casserole as there are cooks, but these two approaches—one with beer, an "after a winter day in the garden or shooting" style—and the other more suitable for a dinner party are favorites.

I enjoy baked potatoes with this casserole, but of course you will need two ovens for that, as they would never cook at 300°F and microwaved baked potatoes are, at the best, a waste of good food. My second choice would be mashed potatoes or creamed potatoes and celeriac (see page xviii) with steamed carrots and/or brussels sprouts or, if you prefer, buttered rutabagas.

2 pounds shoulder of venison, cut into 1-inch cubes

2 tablespoons white flour, seasoned

2 tablespoons olive oil

2 medium onions, chopped

2 garlic cloves, chopped

4 carrots, diced

1 8-ounce piece unsmoked streaky bacon, diced

1¼ cups warm venison or beef stock

1¼ cups dark ale

1 bouquet garni (see page xvii)

4 really small turnips

Salt and freshly ground black pepper

1. Preheat the oven to 300°F and put a dish in it to warm.

2. Turn the cubed venison in the seasoned flour. Heat the oil in either a stainless steel pan or a lidded casserole dish (preferably Le Creuset) and then fry the venison until browned on all sides—about 5 minutes. You may find this easer to do in 2 or 3 batches. Transfer the meat to the warm dish using a slotted spoon to leave the oil in the pan.

3. Fry the onions, garlic, carrots, and bacon in the remaining oil until the onions are golden brown. Add the warm stock, then, as it approaches a boil, add the ale. Let it just come to a boil, then turn down to a gentle simmer. Stir in the meat then scrape up and incorporate all those lovely bits stuck on the bottom of the pan using a stainless steel spatula. Add the bouquet garni and turnips and season well with salt and black pepper. Cover with the lid and transfer to the oven for about 2–2 ½ hours, depending on the quality and age of the venison. Remember if you want to eat at 7:30 p.m., you can put this in the oven 3–4 hours earlier, then remove it from the oven after 1½ hours to check how it is going and return for the last 1½ hours to be finished at 7:30 p.m.

Venison Casserole with Red Wine

There are some magnificently complicated recipes for a venison casserole. Robert Carrier's Magdalen Venison is probably the greatest of them all. I confess I have not yet made it—but one day, or day and a half, I will. In the meantime, this is my workaday recipe to which you may like to add some extras, but I think it is good enough not just for the family Saturday dinner but for a dinner party, too. I usually serve this with creamed potatoes and celeriac (see page xviii) or baked potatoes and a favorite in-season green vegetable.

2 pounds shoulder of venison, diced

2 tablespoons white flour, seasoned

1¼ cups hot venison or beef stock

1 tablespoon olive oil

½ tablespoon butter

1 4-ounce piece streaky bacon, cut into ¼- to ½-inch cubes

1 medium onion, chopped

1 stalk celery, chopped into ¼- to ½-inch pieces

1 carrot, diced

1 garlic clove, crushed

½ cup red wine

4 ounces flat mushrooms, such as portobello or chestnut

1 bouquet garni (see page xvii)

Salt and freshly ground black pepper

For the Marinade

½ cup red wine

1 tablespoon olive oil

1 tablespoon brandy

1 medium onion, chopped

6 black peppercorns

Peel of ¼ orange, in strips

1. Put all the marinade ingredients in a large lidded container and mix together. Add the venison, cover, and leave to marinate for at least 5–6 hours, but preferably overnight.

2. Preheat the oven to 325°F.

3. Remove the venison from the marinade (saving the marinade for the sauce), dry on paper towels, then toss or roll in seasoned flour. Have the hot stock ready for use.

4. Heat the oil and butter in a deep stainless steel pan. Start the bacon frying and then add the onion, celery, carrot, and garlic. As the bacon and vegetables begin to brown, add the venison, which will rapidly take up the oil and butter, so turn the heat down a little and keep turning the meat over to avoid burning. As it really dries out, add the marinade and bring up to a boil, then add the red wine and as much stock as it needs to keep the meat and vegetables covered; reduce to a simmer.

5. Now add the mushrooms. I leave it to this stage partly because if you fry them they will simply soak up all the butter and oil in an instant, and the meat will not have enough in which to fry. If you add more to satisfy the mushrooms, they will release it later in the cooking, and your casserole will be too oily. Adding them at this stage will let them cook slowly and they will take up any spare oil too.

6. If your pan is suitable and has a good lid, you could let it simmer on top of the stove for 1½–2 hours, or until the venison is tender. Otherwise, put the pan (if it is ovenproof, if not, transfer it all into a casserole dish) in the oven for 1½–2 hours.

Venison Meatballs with Tomato Sauce

This is another way to get the best value from the cheaper cuts of venison—
or indeed from a hare, rabbit, or pheasant if you are lucky enough to have
had rather a lot of either of them recently. If you want to bulk this dish out,
it can be served on your favorite pasta—mine is penne. One day I must
try cooking this on top of a layer of pasta—perhaps even with some spinach under the pasta—but I cannot think what to put finally on top. Cheese
sauce? But sometimes my wife suggests why not do something that we know
works well.

For the Sauce

1 tablespoon olive oil

1 medium onion, finely chopped

1 14-ounce can chopped tomatoes

1 pound, 2 ounce–carton passata (sieved tomatoes) or 4 tablespoons
   tomato purée

1¼ cups red wine

2 teaspoons hot pepper sauce (or a mixture of ½ teaspoon paprika
   and ¼ teaspoon chilli powder)

Salt and freshly ground black pepper

For the Meatballs

1 pound venison, minced

1 medium onion (ideally red), finely chopped

2 ounces fresh white bread crumbs

1 teaspoon ground cumin

1 teaspoon ground coriander

1 fresh red chile, deseeded and finely chopped

1 egg, beaten

Freshly ground black pepper to taste

Handful chopped coriander and flat-leaf parsley

Salt to taste (optional)

2 tablespoons olive oil

1. Preheat the oven to 350°F.

2. It is best to start with the sauce so that it can simmer while you make the venison balls. Heat the oil in a casserole dish, or a stainless steel pan with a good lid. Fry the onions until they are soft and golden. Add the chopped tomatoes, passata or purée, red wine, and pepper sauce. Try a taste and add salt and pepper as needed. Then leave it simmering on a low heat. If it threatens to dry out, add a little warm water.

3. For the meatballs, thoroughly mix in a bowl the minced venison (or other game), onion, bread crumbs, cumin, coriander, chile, egg, pepper, and chopped coriander and parsley. I use very little salt but you may want to add a little at this stage. I prefer to combine ingredients like this by hand (even if the phone does always ring when I am doing so). You could use a food processor, but it is easy to overdo it and lose the texture (and it is something to get out, wash up, and put away). Anyway, you have to use your hands to form balls—no bigger than golf balls.

4. Heat the oil in a big frying pan and fry the meatballs in batches, if need be, until they are nicely browned all over. Put them onto paper towels to take off any surplus oil, then place in a casserole dish with the sauce. Make sure the lid is firmly on, then put them in the oven for 40–45 minutes, by which time they should be cooked through and the sauce nicely thickened.

5. Serve straight onto plates, over pasta if you are using that.

Venison with Fruit & Spices

This recipe owes something to the North African tagines, usually of chicken, lamb, or goat. If you want to go overboard with the Moroccan connection, you could serve it with couscous. If you feel more North European—or even British—I think mashed or creamed potatoes go rather well. Venison has become expensive, but you don't need the best cuts for this recipe. Shanks are ideal, but it pays to sever the sinews so that the meat readily falls off the bone when cooked, so make some deep cuts down the length of the shanks.

2 teaspoons salt

½ teaspoon freshly ground black pepper, divided

2 teaspoons paprika, divided

4 venison shanks

3 tablespoons olive oil, divided

2 medium onions, chopped

3 garlic cloves, chopped

Small handful mint, chopped, divided

½ teaspoon allspice

2 teaspoons ground coriander

1½ teaspoons ground ginger

2 teaspoons cumin

½ teaspoon ground cinnamon

2 cups beef stock

A big glass red wine

4 heaping tablespoons tomato purée

8 ounces carrots, sliced lengthwise

8 ounces butternut squash flesh, diced

8 ounces ready-to-eat dried apricots

Juice of 1 lemon

½ teaspoon cayenne pepper

1. Preheat the oven to 325°F and put a lidded casserole dish (preferably Le Creuset) in to warm.

2. Mix the salt, half of the black pepper, and 1 teaspoon of the paprika in a small bowl and rub the mixture into the shanks and into the cuts. Heat half the oil in a heavy pan and brown the shanks. Remove and set aside in the warm casserole dish.

3. Add the remaining oil and cook the onions and garlic until golden and soft. Add half of the mint, the rest of the pepper and paprika, and the allspice, coriander, ginger, cumin, and cinnamon and mix well into the onion and garlic. Add the stock, red wine, and tomato purée, and bring it all to a boil. Pour this mixture over the venison.

4. Put the casserole dish into the oven for 2–2 ½ hours, then bring it out and stir in the carrots, butternut squash, and apricots, then the lemon juice, the remainder of the mint, and the cayenne pepper. Return to the oven for another 30 minutes or until the meat is falling from the bone and the vegetables are done.

Crusted Loin of Venison

Loin of herb-crusted venison with smoked bacon, spring onions, and sage mash, served with warm Cumberland sauce, is a recipe from Jeremy Ashpool of Jeremy's Restaurant, Borde Hill, near Haywards Heath in Sussex, England. It is one of my favorite restaurants. For convenience you could prepare the Cumberland sauce ahead, as it will keep beautifully for up to two weeks in the fridge. Ashpool also cooks a wonderful confit of duck, but you will have to go there to try that.

You will need a good game dealer or a friendly butcher to prepare a good piece of loin cut from the saddle for this quickly prepared dish. Even with minimal hanging, a nicely cooked piece of venison fillet will cut like butter. The secret is simply not to overcook it. A little wilted spinach would be an attractive additional vegetable to serve with the dish.

For the Cumberland Sauce

1 lemon, pared

1 orange, pared

4 heaping tablespoons good-quality redcurrant jelly

4 tablespoons port

1 heaped teaspoon Dijon mustard

juice of whole orange

juice of ½ lemon (discard remainder)

1 teaspoon ginger, freshly grated

A little cornstarch for thickening

1 teaspoon chopped thyme

½ teaspoon chopped rosemary

Half a dozen or so juniper berries, crushed

1–2 pinches sea salt

Freshly ground black pepper

1 pound, 4 ounces venison loin, free of sinew and cut into 4 equal
pieces

2 or 3 tablespoons olive oil, for frying

For the Mashed Potatoes

1 pound potatoes, peeled and cut into regular-size pieces

4 slices unsmoked back bacon, chopped

6 sage leaves, chopped

1 bunch spring onions, chopped

½–1 tablespoon unsalted butter

A little single cream (optional)

Salt and freshly ground black pepper

A little freshly grated nutmeg

1. First, prepare the Cumberland sauce. Blanch the thinly pared rind of the orange and lemon to remove bitterness.

2. Stir the redcurrant jelly into the port over a gentle heat in a small saucepan. When melted, add the mustard and orange and lemon juices. Finally add the ginger and the rind. A little cornstarch and water whisked together and added to the sauce will give a coating consistency if you like a thicker sauce. Simmer for 10 minutes or so, then set aside. While traditionally served cold, there is no reason why this great British sauce should not be served warm as an accompaniment to a hot dish.

3. Mix the thyme, rosemary, juniper berries, and salt and pepper for the venison, coat the pieces lightly in the mixture, and set them aside to allow them to take on the flavors.

4. Preheat the oven to 350°F.

5. Put the potatoes in a saucepan of water and boil as for normal mashed potatoes. Set aside (with a lid on top of the pan to keep the heat in) until the meat is resting for a few minutes after cooking.

6. The cooking of the venison could not be simpler. Heat the oil in your favorite frying pan until almost smoking hot and seal the pieces of meat on all sides. Remove from the stove and place the venison in a moderate oven for 6–8 minutes, depending on how rare you like your meat. Allow the meat to rest for a few minutes after cooking while you finish the potato dish, covering to keep warm.

7. Gently fry the diced bacon in a heavy-based saucepan. Add the sage leaves and spring onions and stir together with a wooden spoon. Pass the potato through a potato ricer or mouli into a bowl, adding the butter and a little cream, if you wish. Add the potato to the mixture in the saucepan and season to taste with salt, pepper, and nutmeg.

8. Slice each piece of meat into 3 or 4 pieces and serve on plates warmed in the oven. Reheat the Cumberland sauce, unless serving cold. Either serve the vegetables and sauce separately or arrange on the plates restaurant style.

RABBIT

[Oryctolagus cuniculus]

Rabbit is good food and good sport.

LIKE MOST GAME, RABBIT IS BEST CASSEROLED, and for my money with mustard and cream in the French style. In general allow about eight ounces of rabbit per head as a minimum, although I reckon four people could manage a whole skinned and cleaned rabbit of about three pounds.

There are those people who prefer cultivated to wild rabbits, and it is a source of endless amusement to me to read the views of those titans of the kitchen, Jane Grigson and her daughter, Sophie. Grigson junior has no doubts: "I'm not too keen on wild rabbits. I don't like the flavor as much and it is tough—I'd rather have domesticated rabbits any day." Grigson senior is just as robust: "Good wild rabbit is a luxury. Domestic rabbit by contrast is as insipid as a battery chicken, even nasty in texture and taste." Well, cooking is art more than science!

Rabbit Terrine

People do not seem to make terrines at home very much these days, although they seem to be popular enough on restaurant menus. That is a pity, as they are not difficult to prepare. This recipe is simple enough, but it is best if eaten a couple of days after being made, so if you intend to eat it on Sunday, you will need to start to prepare it on Thursday. You will need a heavy terrine dish (Le Creuset, of course) with a lid, or use an ovenproof baking dish of roughly the same dimensions—12 ½ x 4 x 4 inches.

> 2 pounds, or thereabouts, boned rabbit
>
> 1 pound fat belly of pork, boned with the rind off
>
> 1 teaspoon fresh parsley
>
> 3 sprigs fresh thyme
>
> 3 or 4 bay leaves, divided
>
> Salt and freshly ground black pepper
>
> 1 bottle white wine (that is, 2 cups for the recipe and the rest for the cook)
>
> 8 ounces streaky bacon slices, half chopped and half in whole slices

1. Place the rabbit and belly of pork in an earthenware dish, add the herbs, 1 of the bay leaves, a little salt, and a lot of black pepper and cover with the wine. Cover with plastic wrap (not foil) and leave to marinate overnight.

2. The following day, preheat the oven to 300°F. Remove the rabbit and pork from the marinade, and reserve the marinade.

3. Mince the rabbit, the pork, and the chopped bacon separately in a mincer, if you have one, or process it in a food processor. Put the meats into the terrine in alternate ½- to ¾-inch-thick layers and cover with the bacon slices. Use the remaining bay leaves as decoration.

4. Pour in as much of the marinade as you can. Put the lid on the dish and, if it is not a good fit, line with foil, but be sure to pierce it below the steam hole in the lid. Put in the oven for 3 hours, then remove and leave to cool slowly. Ideally, keep in the fridge for a couple of days before using.

Rabbit Casserole

This rabbit casserole/rabbit stew recipe is also the recipe for a rabbit pie filling. As always you can work from the basic recipe below, which uses cider, or you can substitute dry white wine or beer. The choice of herbs—particularly the amounts you use—is simply a matter of what you like best. So try it this way first and then develop your own *lapin de la maison*. Vegetables are a matter of choice. Baked potatoes would go well with the casserole as would your favorite winter root or green vegetable for both the casserole and the pie.

White flour, enough for covering the rabbit and a little for thickening the sauce

1 young rabbit, skinned and jointed

2 tablespoons olive oil

1 medium onion, finely chopped

1 cooking apple, preferably tart, peeled, cored, and diced

1 teaspoon chopped thyme

1 teaspoon freshly grated nutmeg, more if you like nutmeg, less if you're not keen on it

1 bay leaf

1 8-ounce piece streaky bacon (I prefer unsmoked), cut into ½-inch cubes

1¼ cups dry cider

1 tablespoon butter

Salt and freshly ground black pepper

1. Season a little of the flour with some salt and pepper and roll the jointed rabbit in it on a plate—or shake it all up in a plastic bag.

2. Heat the olive oil in a deep stainless steel pan with a lid. Gently fry the onions and apples, then remove with a slotted spoon to a plate. Sprinkle over the thyme and nutmeg and add the bay leaf.

3. Fry the rabbit and bacon in the remaining oil until lightly brown. Add the cider—bring it just up to a boil while scraping and incorporating all those sticky bits off the bottom of the pan, then immediately reduce to a simmer and add the apples, onions, thyme, nutmeg, and bay leaf into the pan. Season to taste with salt and pepper, then simmer for 1½–2 hours until the rabbit is tender.

4. In the meantime, gently warm and soften the butter in a saucepan and add the rest of the flour just a little at a time, stirring it with a wooden spoon to make a smooth, thick paste. Remove the meat with a slotted spoon and place it on a warmed serving dish (if you want to serve it smartly) or into a warmed container (if not). Let the stock bubble away while you add the butter and flour mixture (or beurre manié if you are a Francophile) little by little, stirring with a wooden spoon to make a thickened sauce.

5. For the smart dinner option, pour the sauce over the meat on the serving dish. Otherwise put the meat back in the pan and serve directly from that.

Rabbit Pie

1 pound shortcrust pastry (homemade if you want, but chilled or
thawed frozen pastry is fine)

1 recipe Rabbit Casserole, thickened with the beurre manié after 1½
hours of cooking (see page 96)

1. Roll out the pastry to a bit larger than the pie dish. Put the dish upside
down on the pastry and first cut a shape about ¾ inch bigger than the dish
all around. Then cut the pastry to the size of the dish and remove the dish.
You now have the pie top plus a strip of pastry for the rim.

2. Put the thickened casserole mixture into the pie dish. (I like to put a pie
funnel in the dish to hold up the middle of the pastry.) Dampen the rim
of the dish and press the strip of pastry that you cut onto the rim. Now
dampen that and the pastry lid and put that over the pie and press down
around the edge. The pie funnel will make a steam hole in the middle of the
pastry, but if you're not using a funnel, just cut a hole with a knife. If you
are not exhausted by now, you might try using some of the leftover pastry
to decorate the top of the pie—or ask the children to cut it into flowers or
bunnies to decorate it.

3. Put the pie in the oven for 30 minutes or so to brown the pastry.

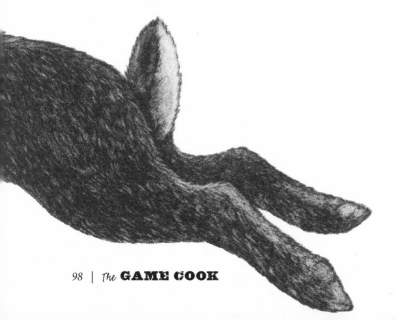

Rabbit with Saffron Rice

This recipe is based on one I found fifty years ago in a Penguin paperback *Plats du Jour,* which remains to this day my (recovered and rebound) bible on risotto. I include it because it is just that bit different—and the recipe for the saffron rice is really rather useful.

1 young rabbit, skinned and jointed

1 small onion

1 bay leaf

Juice of ½ lemon

1 stalk celery, chopped

½ teaspoon thyme

Salt and freshly ground black pepper

1–1½ cups Arborio rice

½ teaspoon saffron threads

1-inch piece mace

2 cloves

1-inch piece cinnamon stick or ½ teaspoon cinnamon powder

1 tablespoon butter, plus a little extra for the rice

⅓ cup white flour

½ bottle dry white wine

½ cup single cream

1. Put the rabbit, onion, bay leaf, lemon juice, celery, thyme, and a little salt and pepper into a large stainless steel saucepan and cover with water. Bring to a boil, then reduce to a gentle simmer for about 1½ hours or so to cook the meat until it can be stripped from the bones. Strain the stock and keep warm. Strip the meat and put it in a warm oven on a serving dish and cover with foil.

2. To cook the rice, use a large saucepan, not only to have enough water but to lessen the chance of it boiling all over the stove. Bring to a boil. Add the rice, saffron, mace, cloves, cinnamon, and a little salt. Bring the water back to a boil, give it all one good stir, and reduce to a fairly fast simmer, it should be done in about 15–20 minutes, but cooking time for rice varies, so always read the instructions on the packet. Put a dish for the rice into the oven to warm.

3. In the meantime, melt the butter in a heavy-based saucepan and stir in the flour to form a smooth paste. Warm the wine gently in another pan and add to the paste a little at a time, stirring all the time to avoid lumps. Then stir in 1¼ cups of the warm rabbit stock. As the rice is finishing, add the cream to this sauce, then keep it over a low heat.

4. Drain the rice—add a dash of olive oil or a little butter—and put into the warm dish.

5. When all is ready, pour the sauce over the rabbit and serve with the rice around it.

Rabbit with White Wine & Mushrooms

I like cooking with mushrooms—anything from sliced field mushrooms fried in olive oil and butter to go with calves liver and onions, to mushrooms in rich shin of beef and oxtail stews. They also go well with rabbit.

The choice of mushrooms is a matter of taste. I buy what looks good in the supermarket (except when I rustle up courage to pick the porcini in my garden). The chestnut mushrooms and portabellos are particularly good and the basic flat mushrooms are perfectly adequate, but I do not have much time for those little white jobs. Also, in this recipe you can very well use dry cider rather than wine. Giving a precise cooking time for rabbit is not easy. The advantage of this dish is that it can be cooked during the day until it is almost done and finished off for the last ½ hour in time for dinner.

Serve the rabbit with a little parsley for decoration and croutons or with some mashed potato and seasonal vegetables.

> White flour, enough to cover the joints, plus a little extra for thickening (optional)
>
> Salt and freshly ground black pepper
>
> 1 young rabbit, jointed
>
> 1 tablespoon olive oil
>
> 1 tablespoon butter
>
> 1 8-ounce piece streaky bacon, cut into ¼-inch cubes
>
> 2 medium onions, chopped
>
> 1 pound mushrooms, sliced
>
> 1 big glass of dry white wine or cider
>
> 2 garlic cloves, finely chopped or crushed
>
> 1 bouquet garni (see page xvii)
>
> About 1¼ cups lamb stock (or better still, rabbit stock from the bits and pieces)—use a cube if you must
>
> Parsley sprigs for garnish

1. Preheat the oven to 325°F.

2. Season the flour with some salt and pepper and roll the rabbit joints in it on a plate—or shake it all up in a plastic bag. Heat the oil and butter in a large stainless steel saucepan and brown the rabbit, bacon, and onions gently. When the rabbit is browned on all sides and the onions golden and soft, add the mushrooms, wine or cider, garlic, bouquet garni, and stock. Let it all come just to a boil, then turn down to a fast simmer. Then, while it is bubbling, make sure to scrape all those lovely brown bits sticking to the pan (I have a favorite stainless steel spatula for this).

3. Then if the stainless steel pan is ovenproof and has a lid, put it into the oven. If not, transfer the contents to a casserole dish. Either way, make sure the rabbit is just covered by the stock. Let it all simmer for about 2 hours or until the meat is tender. Toward the end of the cooking time, put a serving dish for the rabbit and serving plates into the oven to warm.

4. When the rabbit is cooked, remove it and everything else to the serving dish and keep warm while you reduce the liquid by boiling until you have the right amount to pour over the rabbit. Of course, if you wish, you could thicken the sauce, instead of reducing, by stirring in a little flour (I always use a flour shaker for this to avoid getting lumps)—or, better still, add bits of a beurre manié (see page 97) with a wooden spoon.

5. Garnish with parsley and serve.

Rabbit with Two Mustards & Cream

This is a really straightforward recipe—but it is my favorite way of eating rabbit. A decent-size rabbit can be stretched to feed six people. It makes a generous meal for four, but remember that a wild rabbit is leaner and stronger in flavor and needs a little longer, slower cooking than a tame one. I think this goes well with mashed or creamed potatoes and celeriac (see page xviii) and some steamed young carrots.

1 young rabbit, skinned and jointed into 6 pieces

White flour

Salt and freshly ground black pepper

2 tablespoons olive oil

1 tablespoon butter

1 4-ounce piece fat bacon, diced, or same weight of fat back slices

4 large or 6 small shallots, chopped

1 bouquet garni (see page xvii)

1¼ cups game stock (see page xvi) or chicken stock

½ cup dry white wine

2 tablespoons Dijon mustard

1 really heaping teaspoon dry English mustard powder

1¼ cup heavy cream

1. Cut up the rabbit (or get the butcher to do it). This will give you the 4 legs, the rib cage, and the saddle, which is best cut into 2 portions (or even 3). The floppy belly bits can be trimmed off and used for stock. To do a really good job, do not just get it skinned but take off the very thin underskin—but do not spend too much time on that if you're in a hurry. It is a counsel of perfection.

2. Preheat the oven to 325°F (optional, see method below). Season the flour with some salt and pepper and roll the rabbit joints in it on a plate—or shake it all up in a plastic bag.

3. Heat the olive oil and butter in a large stainless steel saucepan and fry the rabbit pieces on all sides together with the bacon or fat back slices. Add the shallots, bouquet garni, stock, and wine, bring briefly up to a fierce bubbling heat, then turn down to a simmer, put on the lid. and cook until the rabbit is tender—about 2–2 ½ hours. Alternatively, put the pan in the oven (or decant the contents into a casserole and put that in the oven) for the same time. Check during cooking to make sure the rabbit is not drying out. If need be, add a little boiling water.

4. When the rabbit is done, remove it from the pan or casserole dish with a slotted spoon and keep warm. Spoon off any excess fat from the sauce. Thoroughly mix the two mustards into the cream and add to the sauce in the casserole dish and warm through gently.

5. Return the rabbit to the pan or casserole dish, make sure it is all thoroughly warmed through and serve.

Roast Rabbit

I loved roast rabbit as a child during the wartime (and postwar) rationing, but it seems rather unfashionable these days. However, I cannot remember if my mother stuffed the rabbit. In any event, you should make sure your rabbit is not an old one. The best indicator of the age of a rabbit is the ears: If young, they can be torn. Also the older the rabbit, the tougher and more leathery its feet will look. In any case, to be on the safe side, you should cook longer at a lower temperature rather than trying a quick high-temperature route. Lastly, I think that a forcemeat stuffing helps to keep it all moist and keeps it from drying out. Serve with mashed potatoes and in winter, roast parsnips or mashed rutagaga, and in summer, broad beans.

1 young rabbit, cleaned, gutted, and inner skin removed

8 ounces fat belly of pork or bacon slices

For the Forcemeat Stuffing

4 ounces bacon or ham, finely chopped

2 ounces shredded suet

1 medium onion, chopped

Finely grated zest of ½ lemon

1 teaspoon chopped parsley

1 teaspoon chopped thyme

Salt and freshly ground black pepper

6 ounces fresh white bread crumbs

4 ounces sausage meat

2 eggs, well beaten

1. Preheat the oven to 350˚F.

2. For the forcemeat stuffing, mix the chopped bacon or ham, suet, onions, lemon zest, and herbs in a bowl. Season well with salt and pepper, add the bread crumbs and sausage meat, and blend together. Then beat the eggs and blend them in too.

3. Now stuff the rabbit with the forcemeat stuffing. This can be quite a game depending on how the rabbit was butchered, and you will probably need a large needle, tough thread, and more ability as a seamstress than I enjoy. Any stuffing that will not stay in the rabbit can be cooked as forcemeat balls.

4. Wrap the pork slices around the rabbit (using cocktail sticks to hold in place if necessary), put on a rack in a roasting pan, and cook for 25–30 minutes per pound total weight including the stuffing, with any surplus stuffing in balls under the rack.

Rabbit with Prunes

[Lapin aux Pruneaux]

I discovered from a Belgian friend that rabbit is enjoyed over there casseroled in white wine and, of course, with cream and mustard. But this recipe, given to me by Madame Micheline George-Maréchal, for rabbit with prunes is rather different. The meat marinates overnight, so start this recipe the day before you want to eat it.

    1 young rabbit, skinned and jointed

    3 medium onions, sliced, divided

    1 carrot, sliced

    1 stalk celery, cut into chunks

    1 garlic clove, sliced

    2–3 thyme sprigs (dried if fresh is unavailable)

    1–2 bay leaves

    3¼ cups pints brown ale or stout

    2–3 tablespoons white wine vinegar

    6 ounces smoked or unsmoked bacon, cut into lardoons

    1 tablespoon lard or 3 tablespoons sunflower oil

    2 tablespoons white flour

    12–15 prunes

    2 tablespoons sugar

    Salt and freshly ground black pepper

1. Place the rabbit in an earthenware dish and cover with 1 of the sliced onions and the carrots, celery, garlic, thyme, and bay leaves, together with the beer and vinegar. Cover with plastic wrap (not foil) and leave to marinate overnight. The following day, strain the mixture through a colander, but reserve the marinade. Remove the carrot and celery and dry the pieces of rabbit on paper towels.

2. Heat a large stainless steel saucepan and fry the bacon until slightly brown, then remove from the pan. Add the lard or oil and fry the remaining sliced onions until transparent, then place them with the bacon.

3. Adding a little more lard or oil if necessary, add the pieces of rabbit to the pan and sprinkle in the flour. Toss and turn the pieces until slightly golden. Add the previously cooked onions and bacon and pour the marinade (including the raw sliced onion) over the rabbit pieces. Add the prunes and sugar, and mix everything well before simmering gently with the lid on for about 1 hour, until the rabbit is tender.

4. Halfway through the cooking time, remove the prunes to a plate and take out the stones (unless already pitted). Squash the prunes with a fork and return them to the pan, then mix everything well for a delicious sauce.

5. Season with salt and pepper to taste and serve.

HARE

[Lepus europaeus]

*Mad as a march hare
but good to eat.*

THE EUROPEAN BROWN HARE (*Lepus europaeus*) is larger than the rabbit, weighing some seven to ten pounds. Living and nesting aboveground on grassland, its prime defense is its sheer speed of forty-five miles per hour and remarkable maneuverability.

There is an awful lot written about cooking hares, but I suspect that not many hares are eaten, and most people have never eaten it at all. Strangely the hare (alongside the pig, camel, and badger) is one of the six mammals regarded as not kosher by practicing Jews. There is also a certain mystique about cooking hare, not the least of which is the ritual use of the animal's blood and the mystery of jugged hare.

Well, it is an attractive creature, but so are many—particularly the wild ones—of the animals we eat. As to the culinary mysteries of the hare—well, read on. As usual it is not so arcane as you may have been led to believe, but do watch out for that inner skin, or membrane. Like rabbits, hares have a second tightly fitting transparent skin, which should be removed before cooking. It is easy enough to peel away, and if you do not do so it will rather spoil the dish.

Roast Hare

Weighing in at ten pounds, a hare is certainly big enough to roast, but usually the legs are reserved for casseroled dishes and only the saddle is roasted. This can be something of a problem, since one saddle is enough for only two people. That is great if you are intent on an intimate meal with the one who means most to you, but not so good for the more usual meal for four people. It may be that your butcher will sell you two saddles or that a farming friend will let you have two whole hares. If not, here is a recipe for two using one saddle, but if you leave it attached to the rear legs you will have a meal for at least four (indeed up to six). In that case, simply double the ingredients for the sauce.

This will go well with my favorite creamed potatoes and celeriac (see page xviii). You might like to add a purée of chestnuts or a green vegetable such as broad beans or very young brussels sprouts (again you will find them at better supermarkets). Elizabeth David suggests beets, cooked as usual, then chopped and reheated with butter and seasoning and a touch of vinegar. I have not tried this, but who am I to argue with that great lady? This will serve 2 (or 4–6 with the legs).

1 saddle hare (or saddle plus 4 legs)

4 (or 8) streaky bacon or fat belly of pork slices

1 tablespoon brandy (optional)

½ cup heavy cream

A small amount hare stock if you have it, or use a lamb stock cube

A little plain flour for thickening

1–2 tablespoons port

1 tablespoon redcurrant or rowan jelly

Salt and freshly ground pepper

1. Preheat the oven to 425°F if you are satisfied your hare is a young one. If in doubt, use 375°F. Put the hare on a rack in a roasting pan and cover completely with the bacon or fat belly of pork. Roast at 425°F for 20 minutes for a young hare (the meat will be pink) or at 375°F for 30 minutes for an older one. Obviously, in both cases, if it is a larger piece (i.e. with the legs on), it will take longer—say another 10–15 minutes. Toward the end of the cooking time, put a serving dish into the warming oven or hot water.

2. When the hare is done, remove it from the oven and transfer it to the serving dish. Carve the saddle lengthwise into strips of fillet. If you have cooked the legs too, remove these and cut into legs and thighs. If you want to make this a special dish, you might follow the way roast hare was served at The Carved Angel and flambé the hare with the brandy. In any case, lay the meat on the warm serving dish with the crisp bacon and keep warm in the warming oven or open your main over door wide and put it there.

3. Check the juices left in the roasting pan. If there is a lot of fat, pour a little off, then add the cream, a little stock if it seems short of liquid, a sprinkling of flour, the port, and the jelly to help it all thicken. Season with salt and pepper. Bring all this to a boil in the roasting pan on the stove, stirring well with a wooden spoon, then reduce the heat to a fast bubble and stir to dissolve the jelly (use a bit more if needed to thicken) while scraping up the bits stuck to the bottom of the roasting pan.

4. Once it has thickened, pour the sauce over the hare and bacon and serve.

Jugged Hare

There are arguments over how this rich stew gained the name Jugged Hare, but it is most likely because it was often cooked in a tall earthenware pot—more the shape of a jug than a casserole dish. This could be covered and stood in a pan of bubbling water over a fire to ensure the hare would be cooked slowly. Of course some would argue that if the blood of the animal is used in the cooking, it then becomes a civet of hare. I leave this distinction aside, but I still remember the joy of my brothers and I when through some miracle of backdoor dealings, usually by my grandfather, in the dark wartime years when there was not much to eat, our mother would announce that she had obtained a hare. Seventy years on in these days of plenty, the memory of jugged hare lives with me still. My mother served her jugged hare with mashed potatoes and rutabagas—or even cabbage. I like some forcemeat balls as well. (There is an alternative—perhaps more exciting—recipe for forcemeat stuffing on page 123, which you can use for the forcemeat balls.)

White flour, enough to cover the joints,
   plus a little extra for thickening

Salt and freshly ground black pepper

1 hare, skinned and jointed

2 tablespoons butter, plus extra for thickening (optional)

1 8-ounce piece of streaky bacon, cut into ½-inch cubes

2 red onions, chopped

1 bouquet garni (see page xvii)

Lots of chopped thyme (or 1 teaspoon dried thyme)

1 tablespoon chopped parsley

1¼ cups red wine—or glass of port

Hare or beef stock as needed (optional)

1 tablespoon redcurrant jelly

The liver, blood, and brains of the hare (optional)

For the Forcemeat Balls

4 ounces fresh white bread crumbs

2 ounces shredded suet

Lots of chopped thyme

1 tablespoon chopped parsley

1 egg, beaten

Grated zest of 1 lemon

2 ounces ham or bacon, chopped

1 ounce butter, lard, or—best of all—goose fat

1. Preheat the oven to 300°F.

2. Season the flour with some salt and pepper and roll the hare joints in it on a plate—or shake it all up in a plastic bag. Melt the butter in a stainless steel pan and brown the hare pieces and bacon. Transfer to a lidded casserole dish (preferably Le Creuset).

3. Lightly fry the onions in the remaining fat, then add the herbs, meat, red wine, and some stock as needed. Bring to a boil, then transfer this mixture to the casserole dish with the hare. Add sufficient stock, if needed, to cover the meat.

4. Stand the casserole in a large pan or roasting pan of hot water and put into the oven. This should be cooked—tender enough for the meat to fall off the bone—in about 3 hours. When the meat is cooked, ladle some of the juices from the casserole dish into a saucepan over low heat. You can thicken this sauce by sprinkling in some flour and stirring that in with the redcurrant jelly and a little butter (or cream if you have any spare in the fridge) with a wooden spoon until it comes to a simmer. Alternatively, you can mash the liver and brains with the blood and add this to the pan to thicken the sauce. Do not let it boil. Blood boiling is not recommended anywhere (although these days mine often does) and certainly not in the kitchen. In either case, once the sauce has thickened, return it to the pan and keep warm while you make the forcemeat balls.

5. To make the forcemeat balls, mix all the ingredients except for the butter, lard, or goose fat in a bowl. Form the mixture into smallish balls (about 1 inch in diameter). Melt the butter, lard, or goose fat in a stainless steel frying pan and fry the balls until golden brown.

6. Serve the hare from the pot into good wide soup bowls, accompanied by the forcemeat balls.

MIXED GAME

Game Pâté

You can make a good pâté from a great variety of ingredients, but the basis has to be in the balance of the essential ingredients and the technique of cooking. Provided you get these right, almost everything else is a matter of what is in the fridge and personal taste for garlic, herbs, and texture. By processing some ingredients, such as the liver, hard pork fat, and half the game meat, less than others, the pâté can have an interesting texture.

The liver should be from any feathered or furred game—or pig's liver or, as a last resort, even supermarket chicken liver. Similarly, the meat should be from any feathered or furred game, with venison as an alternative.

More or less the same ingredients can be used for a game pie, but (especially if it is to be served cold) then you should make a jelly of pigs' trotters, the carcass of the birds, and perhaps a knuckle of veal.

This recipe is for a good basic pâté. Once you discover how easy it is, you should experiment to adjust the recipe to suit your own taste. In other words, create your own pâté maison.

Ideally you should cook the pâté in a heavy terrine dish with a lid—preferably a Le Creuset—or two smaller ones, but if you do not have the Le Creuset, use a Pyrex (or similar) dish; but the deeper, narrower terrine dish is better.

    4 ounces liver

    4 ounces hard pork fat

    8 ounces game meat, from furred or feathered game, or venison

    1 tablespoon butter, divided

    1 medium onion, chopped

    1 garlic clove, crushed—I use 2 good-size cloves, but you might prefer
        to use less

About 2 ounces veal or steak (oddments of pie veal or off cuts of fillet steak are ideal)

2–3 bacon slices

1 8-ounces piece fat belly of pork

6 black peppercorns, crushed

6 juniper berries

Bread crumbs (not too fine; I prefer to use fairly fresh white bread— proper bread not the ghastly wrapped plastic stuff; a good thick slice roughly crumbled by hand is best)

1 heaping teaspoon chopped thyme

2 heaping teaspoons chopped parsley

1 egg

1 slug brandy, Calvados, or even port

Salt and freshly ground black pepper

To Decorate

1–2 bay leaves (optional)

2 glacé cherries, halved (optional)

1. Preheat the oven to 350°F. You will want a mixture of textures in the pâté, so put aside the liver, hard pork fat, and half the game meat.

2. Melt the butter in a stainless steel frying pan and gently fry the onion and garlic just until they are soft and golden.

3. Meanwhile, coarsely chop the veal or steak, bacon, belly of pork, and half the game meat, then mince it quite finely in a food processor together with the crushed peppercorns and juniper berries. Put the mixture in a bowl with the bread crumbs and herbs and add the fried onion and garlic. Beat the egg and brandy, Calvados, or port and add that, season with salt and pepper, then gently mix by hand.

4. Now chop the liver, the hard pork fat, and the rest of the game meat (which you've set aside) fairly small— in about ¼- inch bits. Add all this to the other ingredients in the bowl and mix it all up. Use a wooden spoon and your hands to get a good even mixture. Put the mixture into the terrine dish or dishes, packing it in quite firmly. For decoration you can put 1 or 2 bay leaves or a couple of halved glacé cherries on top.

5. Pour a kettle of boiling water into a stainless steel roasting dish, stand the terrine in the water, and cook for about 1¼ hours with the lid on the terrine or a cover of extra-thick (or doubled) foil over the Pyrex dish. You will know when it is cooked because the fat coming out will be clear in the dish with the pâté floating on it. If in doubt, test with a skewer, which should come out clean. To make it look really good, take off the lid or foil for the last 10 minutes so that the top of the pâté browns.

6. The pâté will be improved if you gently press it as it cools by putting weights on top. Replace the foil (if you removed it) first, then put cans of tomatoes or bags of pasta or lentils on top—they all seem to work quite well.

Game Pots

Game pots make an interesting alternative to pâté, using much the same ingredients of mixed game. This is another recipe from my illustrator, Debby Mason, who can cook as well as paint and draw.

> 1 pound, 4 ounces mixed game meat (pheasant, roast pigeon, and a little venison work well)
>
> 4 cloves
>
> ¼ teaspoon ground mace
>
> Salt
>
> 4–5 tablespoons Madeira
>
> 2 tablespoons butter, plus extra for greasing
>
> 1 tablespoon stock, either bird or rabbit

1. Put the meat pieces in a large stainless steel saucepan with the cloves, mace, and a little salt. Just cover with cold water, bring to a boil, turn the heat down, and then, with the lid on, simmer very slowly for about 2 hours, until the meat is tender. Remove the meat (allowing the liquid to drain back into the pan) and chop finely in a food processor.

2. Reduce the liquid left in the pan by about two-thirds then stir in 4 table-spoons of the Madeira and half of the butter with a wooden spoon. Once the butter has melted into the liquid, add the minced meat and stir to make a smooth pâté. If the mixture is thick, add a little more Madeira or a spoon-ful of stock. Season to taste with salt.

3. Spoon the mixture into buttered ramekin dishes. Melt the remaining butter in a small saucepan and pour a little over the contents of each ramekin to seal.

4. Chill in the fridge and serve as a starter with crispy French bread (you can buy pretty good baguettes ready to cook from good supermarkets) and a little green salad. I like arugula and watercress.

SALMON

[Phasianus colchicus]

Good for the table,
good for the heart.

STRICTLY SPEAKING, SALMON IS NOT GAME, but it is a game fish. And until the advent of farmed salmon, all salmon was hunted and caught in the wild. Nowadays I am told there are eighty times as many farmed salmon as wild ones in the world, although how anyone can know that puzzles me.

As we all learned at school, salmon are anadromous, that is they hatch in fresh water, make their way to the sea, and return to freshwater spawning grounds to mate, lay their eggs, and mostly then to die. I was taught that salmon return to the very spot where they hatched to spawn but nowadays there seems some doubt about that.

Sadly there seems little doubt about the effects of salmon farming upon the wild salmon population. It is devastating, and the Atlantic wild salmon is now in serious decline. In Alaska, farming is prohibited and so far the Pacific stock seems to be in good shape.

The problem seems to stem from both the high density of fish and the feeding techniques used. The large amount of uneaten food that has accumulated on the seafloor of salmon pens and the density of the population give rise to disease and leave the fish vulnerable to sea lice, which escaping fish transmit to the wild population.

Farmed salmon is different from the wild fish because it has a different diet and it is said to have less of the omega-3 fatty acids that they (whoever "they" are) say are good for us. According to some reports it may have more of those nasty dioxins, and farmed salmon are fed red coloring, whereas wild salmon obtains their colorant naturally in its diet. Despite all this, the American Medical Association concluded in 2006 that eating farmed salmon is on balance good for us—but, of course, eating true wild salmon is much better.

They (there "they" are again) say, and so does my wife, that I should not eat meat every day, so to help with meatless days, here are three excellent ways to cook salmon.

Salmon in Pastry

I first ate salmon in this style more than twenty-five years ago at the Connaught Grill when I was the minister for shipping at a meeting with Y.K. Pao, the Hong Kong shipping magnate. It was so good that I did not rest until I had ferreted out the recipe and my wife and I cooked it together for ourselves. Some years later I found a very similar recipe in Jane Grigson's *English Food,* published in 1974, reprinted in 1979, but now sadly out of print. I suppose it would not be politically correct to use that title these days!

This recipe sounds a bit difficult, but really it isn't, though you do need to stick to the cooking instructions. Of course you may like to use more ginger or almonds—that is a matter of taste—but I think this way of cooking salmon is an absolute winner. If there is any left over, it is very good cold.

Coordination is needed to get the salmon and sauce ready at the same time. Do not make the sauce too early or cook it for too long or you may find that it will separate. It will still taste just as good, but it looks a bit uninviting. If you have two ovens, you can make the sauce ahead of time and place it in the second oven to keep warm, along with the plates. If you do not have two ovens, start to make the sauce about ten minutes after the salmon has gone into the oven. Alternatively, if you are preparing this for guests and do not want to be in the kitchen while everyone else is chatting (and drinking), you can prepare the sauce up to cooking the shallots, then put it on one side to reheat and add the cream and mustard just before the salmon parcel is cooked. This recipe serves 6.

2 tablespoons butter, at room temperature

1 tablespoon raisins

1 tablespoon blanched almonds, chopped

4 pieces preserved ginger in syrup, chopped

Flour, for dusting

12 ounces shortcrust pastry (homemade if you want, but chilled or
thawed frozen pastry is fine)

2-pound salmon fillet from the tail end, skinned and cut into 2
matching pieces

1 egg, beaten

For the Sauce

3 shallots, chopped

1½ tablespoons butter

1 teaspoon chopped parsley

1 teaspoon chopped tarragon

1 teaspoon chopped chervil

1–2 tablespoons white flour

2 teaspoons Dijon mustard

2 cups heavy cream, divided

3 egg yolks

Salt and freshly ground black pepper

1 teaspoon lemon juice (optional)

1. Preheat the oven to 425°F.

2. Soften the butter in a mixing bowl by beating it a little with a wooden spoon, then stir into it the raisins, chopped almonds, and chopped pieces of ginger to make a paste. This is to stick the 2 pieces of salmon together, one on top of the other, and to go on the outside of the resultant salmon sandwich.

3. Now for what I find is the tricky part. On a work surface lightly dusted with flour, roll the pastry out sufficiently to make an envelope for the salmon. That is, it needs to be more than twice the area of the fish. Once it is rolled out, lay it over a baking sheet with a slightly raised rim and place one of the fish pieces in the middle of it. Cover the fish with half the paste, place the other piece of fish on top, and use the rest of the paste to coat the outside of the salmon sandwich.

4. Now fold the pastry over to encase the salmon completely. The pastry will stick together best if you just dampen (with a finger or pastry brush) one side of the join and press it together really tightly. Close the ends in the same way, then cut a few slashes through the top of the pastry to let out the steam when it is cooking. Thin the beaten egg with 1 teaspoon of water, if you like, and paint it over the pastry to form a glaze. If you feel artistic (or if the children do), any spare bits of pastry could be used to decorate the envelope. They will stick to the glaze, but make sure to glaze them in turn. Put the salmon in the oven for about 30 minutes. Once the pastry is done, the fish will be too.

5. To make the sauce, start by very, very gently frying the chopped shallots and herbs in the butter. I use a small saucepan rather than a frying pan. Do not let it brown, you are really stewing the shallots rather than frying them. Once they are soft, stir in the flour—something between 1 and 2 teaspoons. You will know when it is enough when it forms a shallot-butter-flour paste with neither any butter nor flour absorbed. Gently add the mustard and the cream (save 3 tablespoons to mix with the egg yolks) all the time over a low heat and let it cook for 10 minutes or so. Now beat up the egg yolks and the cream you saved and stir it into the sauce—still over low heat. Do not let it boil—just cook it gently and it will thicken. Add pepper and salt to taste. You may like to sharpen it with a little lemon juice, but that is a matter of taste.

6. Warm a serving dish and sauceboat. Slide the parcel of salmon carefully on to the warm dish without breaking the parcel. Pour the sauce into the warm sauceboat and let everyone help themselves.

Salmon Coulibiac

In some ways this is a way to feed the same number of people as my Salmon in Pastry recipe does, but with half as much salmon. In another way it is a fish pie that is even more upmarket than my favorite one, the Two Fat Ladies' wonderful recipe. As ever, a good fish pie takes a bit of effort, but it is worth it. A coulibiac is a mixture of fish, rice, herbs, onions, eggs, and mushrooms baked in pastry. If you want to avoid pastry, cook it in a pie dish with a bread crumb (just dotted with butter) topping.

I really cannot think of anything to go with this other than a really good fresh mixed green salad. The great Delia Smith suggests foaming Hollandaise sauce. Well, you can if you like, but by the time I have cooked the coulibiac, I have had enough of the kitchen and want to get my feet under the table. Of course, these days Smith might say to buy your Hollandaise at a better supermarket, and I think that is good advice. Serves 6.

2 eggs

1½-pound salmon fillet

2 cups fish stock—or more—see below (optional)

A few peppercorns

1 bouquet garni (see page xvii)

3 ounces basmati or American long grain rice

2 pinches turmeric

1½ tablespoons butter

1 medium onion, chopped

6 ounces mushrooms (button, chestnut, or shiitake—but not flat ones), chopped

1 heaping tablespoon chopped dill or 1½ teaspoons good freeze-dried dill

1 heaping tablespoon chopped parsley

Salt and freshly ground black pepper

1 pound puff or shortcrust pastry (homemade if you want, but chilled or thawed frozen pastry is perfectly all right)

1 egg, well beaten

1. Preheat the oven to 425°F.

2. Put on the eggs to hard boil.

3. First you need to partly cook the salmon. You could bake it for 10 minutes in buttered foil, but, as for all fish pies, I think it best to poach it in a big shallow pan until it is ready to flake. Do not overdo it. You could use just plain water or the fish stock with the peppercorns and bouquet garni, but half water and half white wine will certainly improve it.

4. While the salmon is cooking, prepare the rice. Rice (even good basmati) is so variable that I simply follow the instructions on the bag, but add turmeric to give flavor and color. Do not overcook the rice—if you want it just al dente. (Alternatively, treat it more like a risotto. That is, melt 2 teaspoons butter in a saucepan, fry the rice in it until all the butter is absorbed, then add either hot water or fish stock and the turmeric, a little at a time as it is absorbed, until the rice is swollen up and, again, just to al dente.)

5. Melt the butter in a large stainless steel pan and very gently fry the onions. As it softens, add the chopped mushrooms and keep cooking gently until it is all nicely soft, adding the herbs toward the end. Now put this onion and mushroom mixture, the rice, the flaked salmon, and the chopped hard-boiled eggs into a bowl and mix it well with plenty of pepper and a little salt.

6. The objective now is to encase a sausage shape of this mixture in the pastry. Roll out the pastry sufficiently to cover the salmon and rice mixture. Lay it over a lightly oiled or buttered baking sheet with a shallow rim and lay the salmon and rice mixture in layers to form a loaf or cake shape on it. Fold the pastry over and seal by dampening one side and pressing it hard on the other to make a seam, and tuck in the ends in the same way. Glaze it all with the well-beaten egg (to which, my wife says, add a tiny drop of water).

7. As ever, if you have any bits of pastry left, you might use it for decoration. I am not much good at this, but young children seem to have the knack for it. Cook for 25 minutes, but keep an eye on it to make sure the pastry is cooked but not overcooked.

Simple Salmon

All this needs is a fillet of salmon, a skillet (preferably Le Creuset) and a little olive oil. Pour a little oil onto a plate and turn the salmon in it. Brush the skillet with a little oil and heat until it begins to smoke.

Put the salmon in the skillet, skin-side down first (it is easier to turn it over that way). Depending on the thickness of the fillet, give it about 5 minutes to char or sear the skin. Then with a large stainless steel spatula (the plastic ones are not sharp or rigid enough) under it and another on top, turn it over and cook until it is seared on the outside but not dry or overcooked.

Serve with a green salad or, if in season, green beans or mangetouts.

SCALLOPS & SPIDER CRABS

[Pectinidae family & Maja squinado]

When Debby Mason wants scallops
for dinner, she simply dives for them.

THESE RECIPES ARE BY DEBBY MASON, MY ILLUSTRATOR. She is a keen scuba diver and fisherman, and when she wants scallops for dinner, she simply dives for them, while most of us have to head for the fishmongers or supermarket.

I know that I am stretching the definition of game to include scallops, but they are just too good to leave out. Diver-caught scallops are a must, as they are environmentally sound and each one handpicked. Trawler-dredged scallops tend to be tiny in comparison, and the damage caused by the trawler's bottom gear ripping through the seabed not only causes severe damage to the scallops' breeding ground but also decimates the whole flora and fauna of the seabed, which can take decades to recover.

Mason was trying to find a spider crab to draw, and approached her local "trade" fish market. Unfortunately she was told that they could only supply spider crabs by the ton! A chance encounter in the pub with a local fisherman secured half a dozen beautiful spider crabs, one of which she drew, the rest inspired the recipe on page 140.

Simple Barbecued Scallops with Bacon

No matter what famous chefs may say, in my experience if a scallop is fresh, it will not turn to rubber if overcooked. This makes them ideal for a barbecue, but good results can also be achieved by grilling. Serve with fresh crusty bread.

 2–3 tablespoons olive oil, divided

 4 streaky bacon slices, cut into short strips, or lardoons

 1 medium onion or 4 shallots, finely diced

 2–3 garlic cloves, crushed

 1 tablespoon chopped parsley, divided

 8 fresh whole diver-caught scallops in their shells

 Half stalk celery (remove stringy bits), finely chopped

 ½ tablespoon butter

 1¼ cups cream or crème fraîche

 4 tablespoons brandy or Noilly Prat (optional)

 Freshly ground black pepper

1. Heat 1 tablespoon of the olive oil in a stainless steel frying pan and fry the bacon over high heat for a minute or two to brown, and then reduce the heat and add the onion and garlic. Cook until the onions just start to go translucent, then stir in half the parsley and remove from heat.

2. Open the shells of the scallops and remove the muscle and coral, keeping the cleaned shells to one side. Cut the scallop muscle across the middle, creating two disks, then cut each disk in half. If you like the orange coral, then also cut these in half and remove the tube running through the middle. (Some people prefer not to eat the orange coral, so this is optional depending on your taste.)

3. Add a little of the remaining oil, to keep them from sticking, and a knob of butter to each of the deeper halves of the scallop shells. Add the muscle and coral (if using) and place under a preheated hot grill or on a rack over a hot barbecue. When the scallop and the butter start to brown, add the bacon, celery, and onion mixture to each scallop shell and also add 2 tablespoons cream or crème fraîche. At this stage, as an option, you might like to add a dash of brandy or Noilly Prat. Continue to cook until the mixture starts to bubble and brown. Top with black pepper and the remaining chopped parsley and serve immediately.

Scallops with Figs, Parma Ham & St. Agur

This starter is a dish that St. Agur (whoever he was) would have died for. It serves 2.

2 large ripe figs

8 fresh diver-caught scallops, white muscle only

1 ounce St. Agur cheese

4 slices Parma ham

2 tablespoons grated Parmesan cheese

2 tablespoons balsamic vinegar

Some olive oil for frying and drizzling

Cornstarch to dust

1 tablespoon butter

Freshly ground black pepper

1. Preheat the oven to 350°F.

2. Cut the figs from the stalk end, halfway down. Turn through 90 degrees and make another cut down at right angles to the first to form a cross. Then open the figs gently so they look like lilies.

3. Cut the St. Agur in half and put half in each of the figs and then carefully close them to look like whole figs again. Then, for each fig lay 2 slices of the ham in a cross shape, put the fig in the middle, and use the ham to make it into a parcel (a cocktail stick can help hold it together).

4. Put the figs on a baking sheet (preferably a nonstick one), sprinkle with the grated Parmesan, and drizzle with the balsamic vinegar and a little of the olive oil. Bake for 10 minutes. Do not overcook it: The cooking seems to enhance the St. Agur to the point where it can simply overpower the delicate flavor of the fig.

5. Meanwhile, dust the scallops with a little cornstarch, heat the remaining olive oil and the butter in a stainless steel frying pan, and gently fry the scallops until brown on one side and then flip over to brown the other.

6. Serve with the figs (and a simple green salad), adding a little more Parmesan, black pepper, and balsamic vinegar.

Spider Crab Spaghetti with Chile, Tiger Prawns & Asparagus

The asparagus in this dish is used to add a splash of color and to diffuse the chile. It is interesting that in this dish the different flavor combinations keep changing right through to the last mouthful. Serve with an overchilled crisp white wine.

2 tablespoons butter

2 tablespoons olive oil

2 4-inch-long red chiles, deseeded and sliced across the width

2–3 garlic cloves, crushed

1 pound, 2 ounces fresh spaghetti or linguine

10–12 fresh baby asparagus spears, cut into 1-inch lengths

12 raw tiger prawns

10 ounces cooked spider crab leg meat or white crab meat

Salt and freshly ground black pepper

Juice of 1 lemon or lime

1 tablespoon chile oil

White truffle oil (optional)

1. Warm the butter in a small saucepan until it is a darkish, nutty brown (*beurre noisette*), skim off the froth, and add the olive oil and return to the heat. When the butter mixture is hot, add the chiles and garlic and heat for a minute or so to allow the chile and garlic to infuse. Remove from the heat and set aside.

2. Cook the fresh pasta in boiling salted water for 3 minutes or as instructed.

3. Steam the asparagus for a few minutes over boiling water. (Asparagus cooks very quickly, so ensure that you remove it from the heat while it still has some bite to it.)

4. When the pasta is nearly al dente, reheat the chile and garlic butter and add the prawns. As soon as they have turned pinkish, add the asparagus and the cooked spider crabmeat and heat through gently, then season with a little salt and pepper and a good squeeze of lemon juice.

5. Drain the pasta (leaving a little water still clinging to it) and stir in the chile oil, then mix in the remaining ingredients and season to taste with salt and pepper.

6. Serve immediately on hot plates, drizzled with the white truffle oil (if using) and finished with freshly ground black pepper.

About the Author

Norman Tebitt is a British politician and former member of Parliament who served as a senior cabinet minister in Margaret Thatcher's government. He was also a journalist for the *Financial Times,* as well as a pilot in the Royal Air Force. He lives near London, England.